Supreme Court Watch—1994

Other Books by David M. O'Brien

STORM CENTER:
THE SUPREME COURT IN AMERICAN POLITICS
THIRD EDITION

CONSTITUTIONAL LAW AND POLITICS:
Vol. 1, STRUGGLES FOR POWER AND GOVERNMENTAL ACCOUNTABILITY
Vol. 2, CIVIL RIGHTS AND CIVIL LIBERTIES
SECOND EDITION

ABORTION AND AMERICAN POLITICS
(*with Barbara Craig*)

JUDICIAL ROULETTE

WHAT PROCESS IS DUE?
COURTS AND SCIENCE-POLICY DISPUTES

VIEWS FROM THE BENCH:
THE JUDICIARY AND CONSTITUTIONAL POLITICS
(*with Mark Cannon*)

THE POLITICS OF TECHNOLOGY ASSESSMENT:
INSTITUTIONS, PROCESSES, AND POLICY DISPUTES
(*with Donald Marchand*)

THE PUBLIC'S RIGHT TO KNOW:
THE SUPREME COURT AND THE FIRST AMENDMENT

PRIVACY, LAW, AND PUBLIC POLICY

SUPREME COURT WATCH—1994

Highlights of the 1993–1994 Term
Preview of the 1994–1995 Term

DAVID M. O'BRIEN

UNIVERSITY OF VIRGINIA

W. W. NORTON & COMPANY
New York London

Printed in the United States of America.

ISBN 0-393-03681-2 (cl)
ISBN 0-393-96656-9 (pa)

W. W. Norton & Company, Inc., 500 Fifth Avenue, New York, N.Y. 10110
W. W. Norton & Company Ltd., 10 Coptic Street, London WC1A 1PU

1 2 3 4 5 6 7 8 9 0

CONTENTS

Cases in italics only are excerpted; cases within brackets are discussed and extensively quoted in the chapter introductions.

VOLUME TWO

PREFACE

Changes in the composition of the Supreme Court often bring changes in constitutional law as well. The dynamics of the Court, of course, also change with each new appointee. Major changes in constitutional law and politics, moreover, are not uncommon when there are several changes on the high bench in a brief period of time. The Court's 1993-1994 term opened with the seating of Justice Ruth Bader Ginsburg, the second woman and seventh Jewish justice to sit on the high bench, and the first appointee of a Democratic president in over a quarter of a century. The 1993-1994 term then ended with the retirement of Justice Harry Blackmun and President Bill Clinton having a second opportunity to make an imprint on the Court by appointing Court of Appeals Judge Stephen Breyer.

Supreme Court Watch—1994 is intended to examine the changes and decisions made during the Supreme Court's 1993-1994 term. Besides highlighting the major rulings in excerpts from leading cases, I discuss in section-by-section introductions other important decisions as well as analyze recent developments in various areas of constitutional law. I preview here some of the important cases that the Court has granted review and will decide in its 1994-1995 term. To offer even more information in an efficient format, I have included special boxes titled "Constitutional History," "The Development of Law," and "Inside the Court."

The favorable reception of and comments received on previous editions of the *Watch* have been gratifying, and I hope this 1994 edition will further contribute to students' understanding of constitutional law, politics, and history, as well as to their appreciation for how the politics of constitutional interpretation turn on differing interpretations of constitutional politics. Finally, I am grateful to my cheerful production assistant Ashley Sigrest, as well as for the support of my friend and faithful editor, Donald Fusting, along with that of his assistant, Kate Brewster, and copy editor, Margie Brassil.

D.M.O.
July 1, 1994

VOLUME ONE

2

LAW AND POLITICS IN THE SUPREME COURT: JURISDICTION AND DECISION-MAKING PROCESS

AFTER ALMOST A QUARTER of a century in which Republican presidents made ten consecutive appointments to the Supreme Court, Democratic President Bill Clinton had the opportunity to fill two vacancies. Midway through the 1992 term, Justice Bryon White announced his decision to resign at the end of the term. Appointed by John F. Kennedy in 1962 at age forty-four, Justice White served for thirty-one years on the bench and remained the last appointee of a Democratic president. In his time on the bench, he established a staunch, though by no means uniformly, conservative track record. On some of the most controversial social-civil rights issues, he voted with conservatives. Justice White dissented from the landmark decision in *Roe v. Wade*, 410 U.S. 113 (1973) (see Vol. 2, Ch. 11),[1] and all subsequent rulings affirming a woman's right to have an abortion, as well as authored the opinion for a bare majority rejecting an extension of the right of privacy to protect private consensual sexual relations, in *Bowers v. Hardwick*, 478 U.S. 186 (1986) (see Vol. 2, Ch. 11). Except for upholding Congress's power to enact affirmative action programs, Justice White opposed such state and local programs, unless adopted to remedy specific policies of past discrimination (see Vol. 2, Ch.

---

[1] References to Vol. 1 or 2 are to the author's two-volume *Constitutional Law and Politics* (Norton, 2d ed., 1995).

12). With respect to the rights of the accused and criminal justice matters, he also generally sided with conservatives, dissenting from the watershed ruling in *Miranda v. Arizona*, 384 U.S. 436 (1966) (in Vol. 2, Ch. 8), for instance. Although supportive of First Amendment free speech claims in many cases, Justice White often dissented from the Court's decisions enforcing a rigid "separation of church and state" under the First Amendment's (dis)establishment clause (see Vol. 2, Ch. 6).

In announcing his decision to retire almost four months in advance of the end of the Court's term, Justice White gave President Clinton not only a chance to fill his seat, but ample time to select his successor. Among others on the Court, Justice White reportedly lamented how the televised coverage of the Senate confirmation hearings for controversial nominees—in particular, the ill-fated 1987 nomination of Robert H. Bork and the bitter 1991 struggle over Justice Thomas's confirmation—denigrated the Court. Besides considerations for the Court's institutional prestige, Justice White may have wanted to ensure that Clinton had ample time to pick a suitable successor given the spats over the withdrawal of Clinton's first two nominees for attorney general and the extraordinary battle that had doomed the last Democratic president's opportunity to affect the Court. In 1968 President Lyndon Johnson's proposed elevation of Justice Abe Fortas to the seat of chief justice was defeated when Republicans and conservative Southern Democrats in the Senate forced Fortas to withdraw from consideration. In any event, Justice White's announcement gave Clinton the first of several possible opportunities during his time in the Oval Office to fill seats on the high bench and to shift the Court's direction on abortion, the right of privacy, affirmative action, and religious freedom, among other matters.

For his part, President Clinton immediately announced that he would search for a nominee who possessed "a fine mind, good judgment, wide experience in the law and the problems of real people . . . and who has a big heart." Yet, over three months passed before Clinton finally settled on Judge Ruth Bader Ginsburg as the 107th justice of the Supreme Court. Clinton had wanted a politician—a "consensus builder"—for the Court. But several prominent and potential nominees withdrew from consideration: New York's governor Mario M. Cuomo and that state's chief judge Judith Kaye, as well as the secretary of the Department of Education, Richard Riley. From a list of over fifty potential nominees (including federal judges Jose Cabranes, Jon O. Newman, Amalya Kearse, and Patricia Wald, along with Tennessee's supreme court justice Gilbert Merritt), the president narrowed the contenders to a handful.

In the week before the announcement of his nominee, Clinton vacillated between elevating his secretary of the Department of Interior, Bruce Babbitt—a friend and former Arizona governor—or naming one of two federal appellate court judges, Ruth Bader Ginsburg or Judge Stephen G. Breyer. Environmentalists wanted Babbitt to stay at Interior, and he faced strong opposition from the senior minority member on the Senate

Judiciary Committee, Orrin Hatch (R.-Utah). By contrast, both Ginsburg and Breyer had the support of Hatch and Senator Edward Kennedy (D.-Mass.). Moreover, each had won seats on the federal bench as last-minute appointees of President Jimmy Carter in 1980. Breyer had been serving as chief counsel to the Senate Judiciary Committee when it was chaired by Senator Kennedy, and Hatch had been instrumental in pushing Ginsburg's appointment through in 1980, when Republicans threatened to block all further Carter judicial nominees. At that time, Hatch agreed to meet her at the request of H. Ross Perot, who was asked to arrange the meeting by his Washington tax attorney and Ginsburg's husband, Martin. Ginsburg impressed Hatch then, and later with thirteen years of service on the Court of Appeals for the District of Columbia Circuit, during which time she served with future Justices Scalia and Thomas, as well as Judge Bork. In 1993, though, New York's senator Daniel Patrick Moynihan, her husband, and leaders of prominent women's groups were among Ginsburg's strongest supporters.

After meeting Judge Breyer for a widely publicized luncheon amid speculation that he would get the nod, Clinton met with Ginsburg the next day. He was plainly touched by the charm and strength of the sixty-year-old Jewish grandmother, jurist, and leader of the women's movement in law in the 1970s. When subsequently announcing his selection, Clinton praised Ginsburg's "pragmatism" and called her the Thurgood Marshall of the women's movement. That comparison, however, was initially drawn by former solicitor general Erwin Griswold when, at the Fiftieth Anniversary of the Supreme Court Building in 1985, he observed that "in modern times two appellate advocates altered the nation's course . . . Thurgood Marshall and Ruth Ginsburg."

Born in Brooklyn, Ginsburg went to Cornell University as an undergraduate, where she also met her future husband. Both Ginsburgs went on to the Harvard Law School, but following her husband's graduation and acceptance of a position in a New York law firm, Ginsburg finished her third year at Columbia Law School, where she tied for first in the class. Following graduation, Ginsburg worked as a law clerk for two years for a federal judge, but then could not find a New York law firm that would hire her in 1961 because she was a woman. After two more years working as a research assistant, Ginsburg was hired by Rutgers University School of Law, where she taught until 1972, when she became the first woman law professor at Columbia.

Because no Jewish justice had sat on the high bench in almost a quarter of a century (since Justice Fortas resigned in 1969), Jewish groups welcomed Ginsburg's nomination, while also rejecting the mythology of a "Jewish seat" and emphasizing that her selection was based on merit. Women's groups were also generally pleased, though some voiced concerns about Ginsburg's criticisms of *Roe v. Wade*. In a 1993 speech at New York University Law School, Ginsburg expressed reservations about the scope, though not the result, of that controversial ruling. In her words:

> [W]ithout taking giant strides and thereby risking a backlash too forceful to contain, the Court, through constitutional adjudication, can reinforce or signal a green light for a social change. In most of the post-1970 gender classification cases, unlike *Roe*, the Court functioned in just that way. It approved the direction of change through a temperate brand of decision-making, one that was not extravagant or divisive.
>
> *Roe v. Wade*, on the other hand, halted a political process that was moving in a reform direction and thereby, I believe, prolonged divisiveness and deterred stable settlement of the issue. The most recent *Planned Parenthood [of Southeastern Pennsylvania v. Casey* (1992) (see Vol. 2, Ch. 11)] decision, although a retreat from *Roe*, appears to have prompted a renewed dialogue, a revival of the political movement in progress in the early 1970s. That renewed dialogue, one may hope, will, within a relatively short span, yield an enduring resolution of this vital matter.[2]

Despite that measured criticism of *Roe*, Ginsburg had been at the forefront of the women's movement in law in the 1970s. Besides teaching at Rutgers and Columbia law schools, in the 1970s Ginsburg also served as the director of the ACLU's Women's Rights Project, arguing six (and winning five) important gender-based discrimination cases before the Supreme Court. Ginsburg championed a legal strategy of chipping away at precedents on a piecemeal basis and building on new principles of equal protection that exposed the irrationality of gender discriminations that often resulted in men receiving benefits they would not have otherwise received. Although ultimately failing to persuade the Court to recognize gender as a "suspect category" under the Fourteenth Amendment, Ginsburg was victorious before the Court in *Frontiero v. Richardson*, 411 U.S. 677 (1973), which overturned regulations that discriminated on the basis of gender in confering benefits for dependents of military personnel; *Weinberger v. Wiesenfeld*, 420 U.S. 636 (1975), which struck down a Social Security Act provision that gave greater survivor benefits to women with children; *Edwards v. Healy*, 421 U.S. U.S. 772 (1975), which invalidated a Louisiana law exempting women from jury service; *Califano v. Goldfarb*, 430 U.S. 199 (1977), which invalidated a Social Security Act provision that automatically awarded survivors' benefits to women, but not to men; and *Duren v. Missouri*, 439 U.S. 357 (1979), which struck down a state law exempting women from jury service upon request of attorneys. With little opposition from Republicans and guarded responses during her confirmation hearings, Ginsburg's nomination sailed through the Senate with a final vote of 96 to 3. On the bench in her first term, Justice Ginsburg proved to be an aggressive questioner during oral argument sessions and gave no sign of experiencing the so-called "freshman effect" in undertaking her share of the Court's

---

[2] Ginsburg, Ruth Bader, "Speaking in a Judicial Voice," *New York University Law Review* 67 (1992), 1885.

workload (see "Inside the Court: Justice Ruth Bader Ginsburg's Reflections on Joining the Court.") By contrast, since his appointment in 1991, Justice Thomas has remained the most reticent member of the bench during oral arguments. Indeed, during the ninety-one hours of oral arguments that the Court heard during its 1993-1994 term, Justice Thomas failed to ask a single question.

On April 6, 1994, Justice Harry Blackmun announced that he would retire at the end of the term. The eighty-five-year-old justice had served on the Court for almost a quarter of a century. Appointed as a "law and order jurist" by Republican President Richard M. Nixon in 1970, at the suggestion of Blackmun's high school friend, Chief Justice Warren Burger, Justice Blackmun initially voted with Burger, which earned them the label "the Minnesota twins." But, Justice Blackmun soon asserted his own independence and over the course of his tenure on the bench came to vote more often on social-civil rights issues with the Court's last liberals, Justices William J. Brennan and Thurgood Marshall. Justice Blackmun authored the controversial landmark ruling on abortion, *Roe v. Wade*, 410 U.S. 113 (1973) (in Vol. 2, Ch. 11), for which he received thousands of letters attacking him, including death threats, and of which he repeatedly said he would carry to "his grave." Although *Roe* will overshadow his other opinions, Justice Blackmun handed down several important rulings, including *Garcia v. San Antonio Metropolitan Transit Authority*, 469 U.S. 528 (1985) (see Vol. 1, Ch. 7), on the Tenth Amendment. He also championed the Court's extending First Amendment protection to commercial speech (see Vol. 2, Ch. 5). On most matters of criminal procedure, however, Justice Blackmun remained a steadfast conservative, writing several significant opinions for the Court that cut back on the scope of the Fourth Amendment; for example, see *California v. Acevedo*, 111 S.Ct. 1982 (1991) (in Vol. 2, Ch. 7). The principal exception to his stand on criminal justice matters was a reconsideration of his position on capital punishment shortly before announcing his retirement (as further discussed in Chapter 10).

Justice Blackmun and President Clinton had become friends over the years, attending annual gatherings of the Renaissance Club in Hilton Head, South Carolina. In announcing that he would retire at the end of the term, as Justice White had almost a year earlier, Justice Blackmun gave the president ample time to choose a successor. Clinton in turn took less time in selecting his second nominee to the Court, taking only thirty-seven days in contrast with the eighty-seven days that passed before he announced his first appointee. Clinton, though, once again agonized and vacillated in making his decision. In the end, he finally settled on the noncontroversial federal judge, Stephen Breyer, whom he had passed over a year earlier. Apparently, Clinton picked Breyer because his other top two candidates would have proven more controversial and might have set off a confirmation fight in the Senate.

Clinton had said he wanted a nominee who was an experienced

"politican" with a "big heart," but he again passed over elevating his Secretary of the Interior, claiming that he "could not bear to lose him from the Cabinet." In fact, Bruce Babbitt was the most liberal of Clinton's top three final candidates and would have confronted strong opposition from the Senate Judiciary Committee's ranking Republican, Orrin Hatch. Conservative groups were also certain to come out in opposition to his views and his attack in 1987 on Robert Bork, President Reagan's controversial and ill-fated nominee to the Court. Clinton's other favored candidate and long-time friend, federal appellate Judge Richard Arnold, presented other political problems. Judge Arnold, a Harvard-trained, former law clerk to Justice William J. Brennan, had lymphoma cancer and had recently undergone low-level radiation therapy. While Judge Arnold's cancer was not life threatening, it could have been used as a basis for senators' voting against his confirmation. Clinton cited Judge Arnold's health as the reason for bypassing him, but the judge's record on the federal bench would have invited attacks from both the right and the left. In particular, liberal women's groups were likely to come out against Judge Arnold because of some of his rulings on all-male clubs and abortion rights.

The fifty-six-year-old Judge Breyer was trained as an undergraduate at Stanford and Oxford universities and later received his law degree from Harvard Law School, where he subsequently taught administrative law for over a decade. In 1979-1980 he served briefly as chief counsel to the Senate Judiciary Committee, before becoming a federal judge on the First Circuit Court of Appeals. After graduating from law school, he also served as a law clerk to Justice Arthur J. Goldberg. During that year the justice handed down his controversial and visionary opinion on the Ninth Amendment in *Griswold v. Connecticut*, 391 U.S. 145 (1965) (in Vol. 2, Ch. 4). Unlike that former very liberal justice, however, Breyer was more moderate and much more of a legal technician. Breyer's academic writings, moreover, concern primarily issues of administrative law and regulatory policy. And for that reason the president's advisers anticipated relatively low-key confirmation hearings for Clinton's second nominee and the 108th member of the Court.

INSIDE THE COURT

Justice Ruth Bader Ginsburg's Reflections on Joining the Court

One week after completing her first session on the high bench as the 107th justice, Ruth Bader Ginsburg shared her first impressions of joining the Court in an interview with the Court's public information officer, Toni House, and the managing editor of *The Docket Sheet*, Kathleen L. Arberg. The following is an excerpt from that interview.

Q: Has becoming a Supreme Court Justice changed your life?

A: Yes, indubitably, yes! Have you seen Sally Potter's film *Orlando*? It's based on a novel by Virginia Woolf. The principal character spends a few centuries as a man, and then wakes up one morning, to find she's a woman. She looks at herself in the mirror and says "Same person, just another sex!" But her life becomes totally different, because she's a woman instead of a man, although inside she is the same person. That's what has happened to me. I have gone about my business as a very private person as a law teacher, even as an advocate for women's rights. Now people recognize me in shops, even in movie theaters. Someone recently remarked to my husband, "Your wife reads her mail by flashlight in the movies." True enough, we went to our local movie house not long ago, and while we were waiting for the feature film to begin—I don't care much for commercials and previews—I did take out the day's mail and a flashlight. No one would have paid any attention to my complusion to save time before. . . .

Q: What is your daily routine like, on a day when the Court's not sitting?

A: On most days, I am chained to my desk, but I expect to have a more flexible routine in time. A lot of the Court's work is new to me. One part of the job that's entirely new, and is particularly challenging, is the *cert.* petition review. Some people outside the Court seem to think the *cert.* pool makes it all a piece a cake—that the Justices simply read and follow what the law clerks recommend. But, to quote *Sportin'Life,* "It ain't necessarily so." We read pool memos with care and the judgment that comes with experience. And when in doubt, we do read the petitions and responses. The law clerks are highly intelligent, very able, uncommmonly diligent. They save us hours upon hours of labor, but most of them are also young and in need of the seasoning that experiences in life and in law practice afford. Whenever I think a case may be certworthy, I will do the homework required, and will not rely solely on pool memorandum. Another time-consumer is the death penalty. I had no idea how many hours the Justices spend dealing with death cases. It's hardly just the few cases that are argued each term; it's all the *cert.* petitions and stay applications as well. Every capital case is on the discuss list, and each Justice's chambers is alert for each pre-execution vigil.

Q: Is there a part of you that misses being an attorney?

A: An attorney is engaged in the art of persuasion, and I think that's a prime part of a judge job, too. When you're taking a position in conference, you have an audience, the audience is your fellow judges. And when you write an opinion, you're also trying to be persuasive. Judging is the best job in the world for one with legal training, because you have an obligation to do only what you find is right, in terms of the law, and the people the law governs.

Q: What other characteristics do you think make a judge a good one?

A: It's important to be secure in your own judgment, to be ready to make decisions and not look back. Some of the best legal minds are not the best judges, because they're constantly rethinking a position and won't let an opinion go. A judge should have the attitude, "I can resolve this as well as, or probably better than, the next person. I'm as comfortable as one or should be making the decision, and I'm not going to worry about it constantly after I've made it."

Q: Students of the Court have written a lot over the years about the "Junior Justice Syndrome"–the tendency of some new Justices to take a while to get adjusted, to speak up. Have you thought about this?

A: There's less of a transition for me in two ways. First, I didn't have to move physically. It would be taxing to move one's home while learning a new job. Second, I've been engaged in brief reading and opinion writing for the last thirteen years, so it's not as much of a wrench for me as it would be for someone who has been in another line of legal work.

Source: "Q&A," *The Docket Sheet of the Supreme Court of the United States* 30, no. 1 (Fall 1993).

INSIDE THE COURT
Voting Alignments in the Rehnquist Court, 1987-1992 Terms*

With Justice White's retirement, Chief Justice Rehnquist lost a close friend, valued colleague, and an important ally on a range of issues. As indicated below, during the 1987-1992 terms only Justices Kennedy and Thomas sided on average with Rehnquist more often than did White, who was followed by Justices O'Connor and Scalia. No two were more closely aligned (94 percent of the time) than Justices Brennan and Marshall, though Scalia and Thomas vote together over 85 percent of the time.

	Rehnquist	White	Blackmun	Stevens	O'Connor
Rehnquist	–	80.2	55.5	54.0	79.4
White	80.2	–	62.3	60.8	72.5

	Rehnquist	White	Blackmun	Stevens	O'Connor
Blackmun	55.5	62.3	–	71.2	59.5
Stevens	54	60.8	71.3	–	57.6
O'Connor	79.4	72.5	59.5	57.6	–
Scalia	77.9	68.4	48.7	48.6	70.9
Kennedy	81.2	75.6	58	56.1	79.3
Souter	73.2	73.5	59.4	57.3	75.4
Thomas	81.2	67.7	46.4	43.4	66.8
Brennan	49.9	54.8	77.1	70.7	50.9
Marshall	48.2	54.7	76.3	72.5	49.1

	Scalia	Kennedy	Souter	Thomas	Brennan	Marshall
Rehnquist	77.9	81.9	73.2	81.2	49.9	48.2
White	68.4	75.7	73.5	67.7	54.8	54.7
Blackmun	48.7	58.0	59.4	46.6	77.1	76.3
Stevens	48.6	56.1	57.3	43.4	70.7	72.5
O'Connor	70.9	79.3	75.4	66.8	50.9	49.1
Scalia	–	78.0	68.5	85.9	49.4	46.1
Kennedy	78.0	–	77.5	71.6	53.7	51.2
Souter	68.6	77.5	–	67.1	–	54.6
Thomas	85.9	71.6	67.1	–	–	–
Brennan	49.4	53.7	–	–	–	94.0
Marshall	46.1	51.2	54.6	–	94.0	–

The above voting-alignment scores are averages of the percentages of decisions during the 1987 through 1992 terms in which one justice agreed with another. The percentages for each term were calculated by dividing the number of decisions in which two justices agreed (in either majority, dissenting, or concurring opinions) by the number of decisions in which both justices participated, and thus the number of opportunities for agreement. The percentages for each term were taken from, and may be found in, Table I(B) of the *Harvard Law Review*'s annual review in volumes 102-107 (1988-1993).

B. THE COURT'S DOCKET AND SCREENING CASES

With a docket continuing to grow steadily, the Rehnquist Court has nonetheless pressed ahead in granting fewer and fewer cases plenary consideration. In its 1992-1993 term, for the first time in the Court's history, the docket rose above 7,000 cases. The rapid growth in the docket is due largely to a rising number of unpaid, or *in forma pauperis*, petitions from prison inmates. That in turn reflects the growing prison population as a result of the "war on crime and drugs" and tougher prison sentences.

Rehnquist Court Terms	Total Cases on the Docket	Number of Cases Granted and Decided	Percentage
1986	5,123	175	3.4
1987	5,268	167	3.1
1988	5,657	164	2.8
1989	5,746	146	2.5
1990	6,316	125	1.9
1991	6,770	127	1.8
1992	7,245	116	1.6

The Court heard only eighty-six hours of oral arguments during its 1993-1994 term. It handed down six *per curiam* opinions and eighty-four full opinions in cases (including nine companion cases) given plenary consideration, for a total of ninety opinions. Chief Justice Rehnquist is credited with cutting back on the Court's workload in spite of an increasing caseload. However, due to the dramatic rise in the number of annual filings, the expansion of the Court's discretionary jurisdiction in 1988, and the Rehnquist Court's decision to grant fewer cases review, less than two percent of the cases coming to the Court are now given plenary consideration. By comparison, in 1953, the first year of Chief Justice Earl Warren's tenure, the Court had only 1,463 cases on its docket and decided 76 (or 5.1 percent) by written opinion. Sixteen years later in Chief Justice Warren E. Burger's first year on the bench, the Court faced a docket of 4,202 cases and decided 108 (or 2.5 percent). In the 1985 term, Chief Justice Burger's last term, the Court had a docket of 5,158 cases and decided 171 (or 3.3 percent). The growth in the Court's docket is due primarily to an increase in the number of unpaid petitions, which has almost doubled in the last decade, rising from 2,352 in the 1982-1983 term to 4,792 in the 1992-1993 term.

The overwhelming number of petitions are never reviewed by the justices, since (with the sole exception of Justice Stevens) eight justices—including Justice Ginsburg—rely on "*cert.* memos," written by their collective law clerks, and study, as well as discuss in conference, only those cases that they and their law clerks deem important (see Vols. 1 or 2, Ch. 2).

INSIDE THE COURT

The Business of the Supreme Court in the 1993-1994 Term*

Subject of Court Opinions	Summary	Plenary
Admirality		3
Antitrust		-
Bankruptcy		2
Bill of Rights		9
Commerce Clause		
1. Constitutionality and construction of federal regulation and administrative action		2
2. Constitutionality of state regulation		6
Common Law		1
Misc. statutory interpretation		16
Due Process		
1. Economic interests		2
2. Procedure and rights of accused	1	12
3. Substantive due process (non-economic)		1
Impairment of Contract and Just compensation		1
Indians		2
International law, war, and peace		-
Jurisdiction, procedure, and practice	4	20
Land legislation		-
Patents, copyright, and trademarks		3

Other suits against the government and officials		10
Suits by states		-
Taxation (federal and state)		5
Totals:	5	95

* Note: The categorizations here are adapted from Felix Frankfurter and James Landis, *The Business of the Supreme Court* (New York: Macmillan, 1927). The classification of cases is that of the author, and necessarily invites differences of opinion as to the dominant issue in some cases. For further discussion see, David M. O'Brien, *Storm Center: The Supreme Court in American Politics,* 3d ed. (New York: Norton, 1993), pages 245 and 397. Note that opinions disposing of two or more companion cases are counted, respectively, twice or more. The table includes opinions and cases whether rendered summarily or given plenary consideration, but not cases summarily disposed of by simple orders, opinions dissenting from the denial of review, and those dismissing cases as improvidently granted.

INSIDE THE COURT

Opinion Writing during the 1993-1994 Term*

Opinions	Majority	Concurring	Dissenting	Separate	Totals
Per Curiam	6	-	-	-	6
Rehnquist	10	-	5	1	16
Blackmun	8	7	11	-	26
Stevens	11	8	13	1	33
Scalia	8	17	4	2	31
O'Connor	12	9	1	5	27
Kennedy	10	9	1	-	20
Souter	8	12	5	-	25
Thomas	8	5	8	1	22
Ginsburg	9	9	7	1	26
Totals:	90	76	55	11	

* Court opinions disposing of two or more companion cases are counted only once here, whereas the cases are counted separately in the table in Inside the Court: The Business of the Supreme Court in 1993-1994. In addition, this table includes cases disposed of either summarily or upon plenary consideration, but does not include concurring or dissenting opinions from the denial of *certiorari.*

I. THE IMPACT OF SUPREME COURT DECISIONS: COMPLIANCE AND IMPLEMENTATION

In *Powell v. Nevada*, 114 S.Ct. 1280 (1994), the Court unanimously held that its earlier ruling, requiring probable-cause hearings to be held within forty-eight hours for defendants arrested without a warrant, in *Riverside County v. McLaughlin*, 111 S.Ct. 1661 (1991) (in Vol. 2, Ch. 7), applied retroactively to all other pending cases. (For a further discussion of the doctrine of retroactivity, see Vol. 1 or 2, Ch. 2.) Writing for the Court, however, Justice Ginsburg held that a violation of the forty-eight-hour rule need not always result in a reversal of a conviction, if other factors in a case rendered the violation of the rule a "harmless rule." Justice Clarence Thomas, joined by Chief Justice Rehnquist, dissented from the part of the Court's decision remanding *Powell* back to the Nevada Supreme Court, which had ruled against applying *McLaughlin* retroactively. Remanding the case, in Justice Thomas's words, would "merely require the needless expenditure of further judicial resources" since Powell's underlying claim "lacks merit."

As the Court has moved over the last two decades in more conservative directions in areas of civil rights and liberties, state supreme courts increasingly have refused to follow the high court's construction of federal law and have recognized new rights or extended protection on the basis of state constitutions to claims that the Supreme Court has declined to embrace (see Vols. 1 or 2, Ch. 2, as well as Vol. 1, Ch. 7). Among the recent decisions, in *Torre Jenkins v. Chief Justice of the District Court Department*, 416 Mass. 221 (1993), the Massachusetts supreme court refused to follow the Supreme Court's ruling in *County of Riverside v. McLaughlin*, 111 S.Ct. 1661 (1991) (see Vol. 2, Ch. 7), that following a warrantless arrest individuals may be incarcerated for up to forty-eight hours before being given a hearing to determine the probable cause for their arrest. In *Rick Sitz v. Michigan Department of State Police*, 443 Mich. 744 (1993), the Supreme Court of Michigan likewise departed from the Supreme Court's upholding of Michigan state police's use of sobriety checkpoints under the Fourth Amendment, in *Michigan Department of State Police v. Sitz*, 496 U.S. 444 (1990). When that case was remanded back to the state appellate court, the state court held that the state's policy of indiscriminate suspicionless stopping of automobiles violates Michigan's state constitution's prohibition against unreasonable searches and seizures.

Torre Jenkins v. Chief Justice of the District Court Department

Supreme Judicial Court of Massachusetts
416 Mass. 221 (1993)

Torre Jenkins, who along with several other defendants who were arrested without a warrant on a Friday afternoon and held without an arraignment hearing on the probable cause for their arrest until the following Monday, petitioned the state district court to order that all warrantless arrests be followed by a prompt judicial determination of the probable cause for arrest. The chief justices of the state district court and of the Boston municipal court filed a memorandum in opposition. Subsequently, Jenkins appealed to the Supreme Court of Massachusetts.

The Court's decision was unanimous.

Chief Justice LAICOS delivers the opinion of the Court:

In *Gerstein v. Pugh*, 420 U.S. 103 (1975), the Supreme Court of the United States held that the Fourth Amendment to the United States Constitution mandates the States to "provide a fair and reliable determination of probable cause as a condition for any significant pre-trial restraint of liberty, and this determination must be made by a judicial officer either before or promptly after arrest." . . .

Following *Gerstein*, federal appellate courts disagreed as to how "promptly" a State must provide a probable cause determination following a warrantless arrest. A majority of courts understood *Gerstein* to mandate that such determination be made immediately after the completion of the administrative procedures necessitated by the arrest.

In *County of Riverside v. McLaughlin*, 114 L.Ed.2d 49 (1991), the Supreme Court undertook to define "what is 'prompt' under *Gerstein*." The Court rejected the view that the Fourth Amendment requires a determination of probable cause immediately following completion of the administrative steps incident to arrest. The Court held that principles of federalism demanded that States be given the flexibility to experiment with their criminal procedures. Such flexibility, the Court concluded, encompassed the States' right to delay judicial determination of probable cause in order to combine it with other pretrial proceedings. The Court reasoned that, in order to ascertain the outer time limit to such delay, the State interest in "protecting public safety" should be balanced with the individual's interest in avoiding "prolonged detention based on incorrect or unfounded suspicion." Applying this balancing test, the Court settled on a "practical compromise," whereby "a jurisdiction that provides judicial determinations of probable cause within forty-eight hours of arrest will, as a general matter, comply with the promptness requirement of *Gerstein.*"

Four Justices dissented and expressed disagreement with the Court's conclusion that the administrative convenience of a State justifies delaying the grant of a probable cause determination to individuals arrested without a warrant. . . . After an extensive survey of the relevant authorities, [dissenting] Justice SCALIA concluded that States need no more than twenty-four hours to complete the administrative steps incident to arrest and to arrange for a probable cause determination by a magistrate.

The plaintiffs essentially urge us to adopt as matter of State constitutional law the views stated in Justice SCALIA's dissent. The defendants argue in response that the balancing test followed by the five Justices in the majority provides the construct of constitutional analysis that we should follow under the State Constitution. The defendants contend that, under this balancing test, a forty-eight hour delay between arrest and judicial determination of probable cause represents an acceptable compromise between the competing interests at stake.

Article 14 of the Massachusetts Declaration of Rights, adopted by the people in 1780, provides:

"Every subject has a right to be secure from all unreasonable searches, and seizures, of his person, his houses, his papers, and all his possessions. All warrants, therefore, are contrary to this right, if the cause or foundation of them be not previously supported by oath or affirmation; and if the order in the warrant to a civil officer, to make search in suspected places, or to arrest one or more suspected persons, or to seize their property, be not accompanied with a special designation of the persons or objects of search, arrest, or seizure: and no warrant ought to be issued but in cases, and with the formalities prescribed by the laws."

As we do with other provisions of the State Constitution, we construe the language of this constitutional provision "in light of the circumstances under which it was framed, the causes leading to its adoption, the imperfections hoped to be remedied, and the ends designed to be accomplished." *General Outdoor Advertising Co. v. Department of Pub. Works*, 289 Mass. 149 (1935).

It is well known that art[icle] 14 was adopted to prohibit the abuse of official power brought about by two devices which the British Crown used in the colonies: the general warrants and the writs of assistance. The writs of assistance were a special kind of general warrant which permitted their bearer, usually a customs official, to search with unlimited discretion for smuggled goods without special application to a court.

The crux of the colonists' objection to these legal devices was the unchecked control over the liberty of the people which they vested in law enforcement officers. In the famed Petition of Lechmere, argued in 1761, James Otis presented a theory of American jurisprudence which embodied the colonists' position and formed the conceptual basis of art[icle] 14. "Every one with this writ may be a tyrant," Otis argued. "If this commission is legal, a tyrant may, in a legal manner also, controul, imprison or murder any one within the realm. [Being] accountable to no persons for his doings, every man may reign secure in his petty tyranny, and spread terror and desolation around him, until the trump of the arch angel shall excite different emotions in his soul." Such evils, Otis concluded, would only be remedied if a neutral judiciary controlled governmental interference with the liberty of the people: "An officer should show probable grounds, should take his oath on it, should do this before a magistrate, and . . . such magistrate, if he thinks proper should issue a special warrant to a constable to search the places."

John Adams, the principal author of our Constitution, sat in the courtroom and wholeheartedly embraced Otis's argument. "Otis lost his case, but his side was to win the war. Throughout the colonies, opposition to the writs mounted in the wake of Otis's words, and courts proved increasingly reluctant to issue them."

The language and structure of article 14 reflects John Adams's adoption of Otis's views. Beginning with the prohibition of "unreasonable" searches and seizures, art[icle] 14 moves on to define the fundamental components of a constitutionally reasonable search or seizure: First, magistrates—rather than law enforcement agents—control the decision whether to effectuate a search and seizure, including the seizure or arrest of a person. Second, law enforcement agents bear the burden of justifying their intrusion into a person's freedom by presenting the magistrate with sufficient grounds to support the search or the seizure. These two elements are the essence of the constitutional norm regarding searches and seizures, today no less than in 1780. . . .

We conclude that article 14 embodies the common law guarantee that a warrantless arrest must be followed by a judicial determination of probable cause no later than reasonably necessary to process the arrest and to reach a magistrate. The historical background to the adoption of article 14 evinces the intent of its framers to afford the citizens of this Commonwealth at least as much protection regarding a warrantless arrest as was provided by the common law. . . .

Having concluded that the only element bearing on the reasonableness of the delay between a completed arrest and a judicial determination of probable cause is the time reasonably necessary to reach a magistrate, we turn to the issue of the outermost time limit to such delay. . . .

Every State in the country has a statute or rule governing the presentment of an arrestee to a magistrate for a probable cause determination. A number of States require that such presentment be made within twenty-four hours of arrest: One State requires that it be done within twenty hours. Seven States require that it be done within twenty-four hours. Twenty-eight States and the District of Columbia have statutes requiring presentment or arraignment "without unnecessary delay" or "forthwith." State courts have . . . applied a 24-hour limit under state statutes requiring presentment without 'unreasonable delay.' New York, for example, has concluded that no more than 24 hours is necessary from arrest to arraignment. Only seven States explicitly authorize detention for more than twenty-four hours: Four States have settled on a forty-eight hour time limit, one State on a thirty-six hour time limit, and, before *County of Riverside* undermined the constitutionality of their statutes or rules, two States authorized detention for up to seventy-two hours. One State authorizes detention "one night or longer."

Most Federal cases decided in the wake of Gerstein have concluded that twenty-four hours provides a reasonable amount of time within which to complete arrest procedures.

Our review of these authorities leads us to conclude that there is widespread agreement that the Commonwealth needs no more than twenty-four hours to provide such a determination following a warrantless arrest. We have concluded that, under our State Constitution, the sole element bearing on the delay between a processed arrest and such a determination is the time reasonably needed to reach a magistrate. In light of the data that we have reviewed, we hold that, in the usual circumstance, no more than a twenty-four hour time period is needed to reach the magistrate. In order to accommodate unforeseeable circumstances, we shall treat this time limit as a presumption: Where it is exceeded, the police must bear the burden of demonstrating that an extraordinary circumstance caused the delay.

THE DEVELOPMENT OF LAW

Congress Overrides the Court: The Religious Freedom Restoration Act of 1993

Congress overrode the controversial ruling in *Employment Division, Department of Human Resources of Oregon v. Smith*, 494 U.S. 872 (1990) (see Vol. 2, Ch. 6) with the enactment of The Religious Freedom Restoration Act of 1993. Writing for the majority in *Smith*, Justice Scalia rejected the Warren Court's analysis of the First Amendment's protection for religious freedom in *Sherbert v. Verner*, 374 U.S. 398 (1963) (see Vol. 2, Ch. 6). In *Sherbert* the Court advanced a "balancing test," requiring states to show a compelling interest in regulations that justifies overriding free exercise claims. By contrast, *Smith* held that there should be no exemption from otherwise "generally applicable laws" for individuals claiming they are denied the First Amendment's protection for the free exercise of religion. That ruling angered and united a broad range of religious organizations, who in turn succeeded in pushing Congress to enact the Religious Freedom Restoration Act.

The coalition that pushed for the enactment of the Religious Freedom Restoration Act included liberal, conservative, and religious organizations, such as the National Association of Evangelicals, the Southern Baptist Convention, the National Council of Churches, the American Jewish Congress, the National Conference of Catholic Bishops, the Morman Church, the Traditional Values Coalition, and the American Civil Liberties Union. In support of the legislation, sponsors pointed out that following the 1990 ruling in *Smith*, lower courts had denied exemptions for religious minorities, such as the Amish, in over fifty cases.

The Religious Freedom Restoration Act basically rewrote *Sherbert v. Verner's* analysis and "balancing test" back into federal law, thereby overriding the Rehnquist Court's decision in *Smith.* The act forbids any federal agency or state government from burdening a person's free exercise of religion, even if the burden results from a law of general applicability, unless the agency or state government demonstrates that the regulation or law burdening an individual's religious freedom (1) "furthers a compelling governmental interest" and (2) "is the least restrictive means of furthering that compelling governmental interest."

4

THE PRESIDENT AS CHIEF EXECUTIVE IN DOMESTIC AFFAIRS

B. APPOINTMENT AND REMOVAL POWERS

In *Weiss v. United States*, 114 S.Ct. 752 (1994), the Court confronted a challenge under the appointments clause of Article II and the Fifth Amendment's due process clause to the way judges are appointed in military courts. Article II authorizes the president to

> nominate, and by and with the Advice and Consent of the Senate, shall appoint Ambassadors, other public Ministers and Consuls, Judges of the supreme Court, and all other Officers of the United States, whose Appointments are not herein otherwise provided for, and which shall be established by Law; but the Congress may by law vest the Appointment of such inferior Officers, as they think proper, in the President alone, in the Courts of Law, or in the Heads of Departments.

Under the Uniform Code of Military Justice (UCMJ), a special and general court martial trial is heard before a military judge and from three to five court martial members, all of whom are temporarily assigned by the Judge Advocate General. Weiss, a marine who was found guilty of larceny at a special court martial, appealed on the grounds that the UCMJ's prescribed appointment method violated Article II and the due process clause.

Writing for the majority, Chief Justice Rehnquist rejected the contentions that the appointment as judges of commissioned military officers runs afoul of Article II. Neither did he find any merit to the claim that the position of a military judge is so similar to other positions specified in Article II as to require Senate confirmation, nor did he agree that military judges are akin to other high government officials, such as the Chairman of the Joint Chief of Staff, subject to a second appointment proceeding under Article II. In the chief justice's words: "It is quite clear that Congress has not required a separate appointment to the position of military judge, and we believe it equally clear that the Appointments Clause by its own force does not require a second appointment before military officers may discharge the duties of such a judge."

In addition, *Weiss* laid to rest the claim that military judges' fixed terms of tenure and provisions for independence fall short of ensuring the kind of judicial independence enjoyed by federal judges and required by the due process clause. "Although a fixed term of office is a traditional component of the Anglo-American civilian judicial system," Rehnquist added that, "it has never been a part of the military justice tradition." That historical fact should be accorded great weight, according to Rehnquist. "A fixed term of office," as the chief justice put it, "is not an end in itself. It is a means of promoting judicial independence, which in turn helps to ensure judicial impartiality. We believe the applicable provisions of the UCMJ, and corresponding regulations, by insulating military judges from the effects of command influence, sufficiently preserve judicial impartiality so as to satisfy the Due Process Clause." In separate opinions, Justices Ginsburg, Souter, and Scalia concurred.

C. LEGISLATIVE POWERS IN THE ADMINISTRATIVE STATE

With the collapse of the Soviet Union and the end of the Cold War era, Congress finally agreed on a plan for closing U.S. military bases and getting around the vexing problem of members of Congress fighting to preserve bases located in their home districts and states. Under the 1990 Defense Base Closure and Realignment Act, an indpendent commission was created to hold public hearings, consider proposals made by the secretary of Defense, and to make recommendations for base closings. The president, then, must approve or reject the entire list of proposed closings and Congress has forty-five days to veto his action. Accordingly, neither the president nor members of Congress may remove or add individual bases to the package.

When the decision to close the 193-year-old Philadephia Naval Shipyard was subsequently made, however, Pennsylvania's Republican senator Arlen Specter sued and claimed that it was improperly slated for closure. He also argued that federal courts should review the commission's procedures in order to determine their fairness. A federal district court initially dismissed his suit, but the Court of Appeals for the Third Circuit reversed and the federal government appealed its decision to the Supreme Court.

Writing for the Court in *Dalton v. Specter*, 114 S.Ct. – (1994), Chief Justice Rehnquist rejected Senator Specter's claims of standing to sue under the

Administrative Procedure Act (APA) and on the basis of a constitutional claim. Relying on an earlier ruling, in *Franklin v. Massachusetts*, 112 S.Ct. 2767 (1992), which limited judicial review under the APA to only governmental agencies' "final" decisions, the chief justice dismissed Specter's challenge to the independent commission's procedures. The commission's recommendations were not technically "final," reasoned Rehnquist, since they remained subject to the president's approval. "Without the President's approval," the chief justice emphasized, "no bases are closed under the act." Turning next to Specter's claim that the president had violated the 1990 act by accepting flawed recommendations, Chief Justice Rehnquist rejected out of hand the contention that the senator had raised a "constitutional" claim meriting judicial review. In the chief justice's words:

> Our cases do not support the proposition that every action by the President, or by another executive official, in excess of his statutory authority is *ipso facto* in violation of the Constitution. On the contrary, we have often distinguished between claims of constitutional violations and claims that an official has acted in excess of his statutory authority. . . . [C]laims simply alleging that the President has exceeded his statutory authority are not "constitutional" claims, subject to judicial review under the exception recognized in *Franklin* [*v. Massachusetts*, 112 S.Ct. 2767 (1992)]. . . .
>
> So the claim raised here is a statutory one: The President is said to have violated the terms of the 1990 Act by accepting procedurally flawed recommendations. The exception identified in *Franklin* for review of constitutional claims thus does not apply in this case. We may assume for the sake of argument that some claims that the President has violated a statutory mandate are judicially reviewable outside the framework of the APA. See *Dames & Moore v. Regan*, 453 U.S. 654 (1981). But longstanding authority holds that such review is not available when the statute in question commits the decision to the discretion of the President. . . .
>
> How the President chooses to exercise the discretion Congress has granted him is not a matter for our review. As we stated in [*United States v.*] *George S. Bush & Co.*, [310 U.S. 371 (1940)], "no question of law is raised when the exercise of [the President's] discretion is challenged."
>
> In sum, we hold that the actions of the Secretary and the Commission cannot be reviewed under the APA because they are not "final agency actions." The actions of the President cannot be reviewed under the APA because the President is not an "agency" under that Act. The claim that the President exceeded his authority under the 1990 Act is not a constitutional claim, but a statutory one. Where a statute, such as the 1990 Act, commits decisionmaking to the discretion of the President, judicial review of the President's decision is not available.

In a separate opinion joined by Justices Blackmun, Ginsburg, and Stevens, however, Justice Souter pointed out that,

> It is not necessary to reach the question the Court answers in Part I, whether the

Commission's report is final agency action, because the text, structure, and purpose of the Act compel the conclusion that judicial review of the Commission's or the Secretary's compliance with it is precluded. There is, to be sure, a "strong presumption that Congress did not mean to prohibit all judicial review." But although no one feature of the Act, taken alone, is enough to overcome that strong presumption, I believe that the combination present in this unusual legislative scheme suffices.

In adopting the Act, Congress was intimately familiar with repeated, unsuccessful, efforts to close military bases in a rational and timely manner. That history of frustration is reflected in the Act's text and intricate structure, which plainly express congressional intent that action on a base-closing package be quick and final, or no action be taken at all. . . . While no one aspect of the Act, standing alone, would suffice to overcome the strong presumption in favor of judicial review, this structure (combined with the Act's provision for Executive and congressional review, and its requirement of time-constrained judicial review of implementation under NEPA) can be understood no other way than as precluding judicial review of a base-closing decision under the scheme that Congress, out of its doleful experience, chose to enact. I conclude accordingly that the Act forecloses such judicial review.

5

CONGRESS: MEMBERSHIP, IMMUNITIES, AND INVESTIGATORY POWERS

IN ITS 1994-1995 TERM, the Court will confront the controversial issue of whether states may impose term limits on representatives elected to Congress in two consolidated cases from Arkansas: *U.S. Term Limits v. Thorton* and *Bryant v. Hill.* Since 1990, fifteen states have enacted limits on congressional terms, and there are efforts to do so in several other states. In 1992, Arkansas voters approved an amendment to the state constitution that prohibits the placing on an election ballot the name of anyone who has been previously elected to three terms (six years) or more in the House of Representatives or two terms (twelve years) in the Senate. Opponents of such term limitations, however, argue that they violate Article I of the U.S. Constitution. Article I specifies only three qualifications—relating to age, citizenship, and residency—for holding congressional office. The Arkansas state supreme court struck down the restrictions on incumbents holding office. Term limitations enacted in Washington and Nebraska have also been challenged and invalidated by courts.

6

CONGRESS: LEGISLATIVE, TAXING, AND SPENDING POWERS

WHEN CONGRESS ENACTED the controversial Civil Rights Act of 1991, which overrode numerous recent rulings of the Supreme Court (see "The Development of Law: Congress Reverses the Supreme Court—The Civil Rights Act of 1991," in Chapter 2 in Vols. 1 or 2), it could not agree on whether the law's provisions should apply retroactively to cases pending in the courts. Democrats argued that the law's provisions forbidding gender and racial harassment and discrimination in the workplace should apply retroactively, while Republicans and the Bush administration stood adamantly in opposition. In two rulings in 1994, the Court held eight to one that the Civil Rights Acts of 1991 does not apply retroactively. Writing for the majority in *Landgraf v. USI Film Products*, 114 S.Ct. 1483 (1994), and *Rivers v. Roadway Express*, 114 S.Ct. 1530 (1994), Justice Stevens issued a broad ruling holding that congressional legislation must explicitly state that it applies retroactively, otherwise the courts should presume that it does not. In *Landgraf*, a woman had sued a company in the mid-1980s after a co-worker repeatedly harassed her, which a trial court deemed not severe enough to force her to quit her job, and her appeal was pending when the 1991 law went into effect. In *Rivers*, two black mechanics challenged their firings as racially discriminatory, but before their suits were decided, the Supreme Court handed down decisions narrowing the scope of Section 1981 of the Civil Rights Act. When the Civil Rights Act of 1991 overrode those decisions, then, an appellate court held that the 1991 statute did not apply retroactively, and they appealed to the Supreme Court.

In Justice Stevens's words, "Since the early days of this Court, we have declined to give retroactive effect to statutes burdening private rights, unless Congress ha[s] made clear its intent." After examining the legislative history of the Civil Rights Act of 1991, Justice Stevens observed that, "It seems likely that one of the compromises that made it possible to enact the 1991 version was an agreement *not* to include the kind of explicit retroactivity command found in the 1990 bill."

In a concurring opinion, however, Justice Scalia chided the majority for looking to the congressional history of the 1991 law and engaging in what he deemed "the soft science of legislative history." In his view, the Court should have rested its decision solely on the text of the statute. By contrast, dissenting Justice Blackmun argued that the majority's rulings in the two cases simply "prolongs the life of " the Court's prior rulings, which Congress had expressly repudiated, and insisted that "at no time within the last generation has an employer had a vested right to engage in or permit sexual harassment."

During its 1994-1995 term the Court will consider an appeal of a federal court's decision striking down a 1990 "Gun Free School Zones" congressional statute, which bars the possession of firearms within one thousand feet of any school grounds. The Court of Appeals for the Fifth Circuit, in *United States v. Lopez*, held that Congress exceeded its power under the commerce clause and intruded into an area reserved for state and local governments when enacting the statute. The appellate court, though, conceded that a federal gun-free schools law might be a permissible exercise of congressional power under the commerce clause, but when passing the 1990 statute, Congress failed to make formal findings about the effects of gun use on interstate commerce and to require prosecutors to establish a connection between firearms and interstate commerce before obtaining convictions under the statute. The Supreme Court's ruling in *Lopez*, depending on its breadth, could be very significant and bear on the validity of other recent federal gun laws, including the so-called Brady bill, which imposes a waiting period on the purchase of handguns.

7

THE STATES AND AMERICAN FEDERALISM

A. STATES' POWER OVER COMMERCE AND REGULATION

As usual, the Court took a fair number of commerce clause cases in its 1993-1994 term. (See "The Development of Law" boxes in this chapter.) In particular, and as has become more common since the late 1980s, the Court again confronted challenges to state and local attempts to regulate the disposal of hazardous waste. In *Oregon Waste Systems, Inc. v. Department of Environmental Quality of the State of Oregon*, 114 S.Ct. 1345 (1994), the Court again struck down a state law imposing a surcharge on the disposal of solid waste generated outside of the state's borders as a violation of the dormant commerce clause. Under a 1989 law, Oregon imposed a fee of $3.10 per ton on the disposal of out-of-state waste in its landfills. Writing for the Court, Justice Thomas overturned the law as economic protectionism that unconstitutionally discriminated against interstate commerce. "Discrimination simply means differential treatment of in-state and out-of-state economic interests that benefits the former and burdens the latter," Justice Thomas observed when holding that, "if a restriction on commerce is discriminatory, it is virtually per se invalid."

Chief Justice Rehnquist, joined by Justice Blackmun, dissented and countered that "Oregon should be applauded" for developing a comprehensive plan for its solid-waste disposal problem. "The Court today leaves states with only two options," argued the chief justice, "become a dumper and ship as much waste as possible to a less populated state or become a dumpee, and stoically accept waste from more densely populated states." Concluding, Chief Justice Rehnquist added that, "I see nothing in the commerce clause that compels less densely populated states to serve as the low-cost dumping grounds for their neighbors."

THE DEVELOPMENT OF LAW

Rulings on State Regulations of Commerce in the Absence of Federal Legislation

Case	Vote	Ruling
Northwest Airlines, Inc. v. County of Kent, Michigan, 114 S.Ct. 855 (1994)	7:1	Rejected a dormant commerce clause challenge to an airport fee scheme that discriminated between commerical airlines and general aviation by assessing higher fees on the former. Justice Thomas dissented.
Oregon Waste Systems, Inc. v. Department of Environmental Quality of the State of Oregon, 114 S.Ct. 1345 (1994)	7:2	Struck down Oregon's surcharge on the disposal of out-of-state solid waste in its landfills as discriminatory economic protectionism in violation of the dormant commerce clause. Chief Justice Rehnquist and Justice Blackmun dissented.
C&A Carbone, Inc. v. Town of Clarkstown, New York, 113 S.Ct. 1677 (1994)	7:2	Struck down an ordinance requiring all nonhazardous solid waste within the town to be deposited at a local transfer station. Writing for the majority, Justice Kennedy held that the ordinance deprived out-of-state businesses of access to the local market and thereby unconstitutionally discriminated in favor of local businesses. Chief Justice Rehnquist and Justice Souter dissented.
Associated Industries of Missouri v. Lohman, 114 S.Ct. 1815 (1994)	9:0	Writing for the Court, Justice Thomas invalidated a statewide "additional use tax" on goods purchased outside of the state for impermissibly discriminating against interstate commerce.
West Lynn Creamery, Inc. v. Healy, 114 S.Ct. – (1994)	7:2	Struck down a Massachusetts pricing order on all milk sold within the state and subsidy for in-state dairy farmers as economically discriminatory and a violation of the commerce clause. Justice Stevens wrote for the majority and Chief Justice Rehnquist, joined by Justice Thomas, dissented.

Barclays Bank PLC v. Franchise Tax Board of California and *Colgate-Palmolive Co. v. Franchise Tax Board of California*, 114 S.Ct., — (1994)	7:2	Writing for the Court's majority, Justice Ginsburg upheld a controversial state policy of taxing multinational corporations based on their worldwide income, rather than on their earnings within the state, over objections that the policy discriminates against foreign and interstate commerce. The majority reaffirmed that state tax policies may run afoul of the commerce clause if the tax (1) applies to an activity lacking a "substantial nexus to the taxing state"; (2) is not fairly apportioned; (3) discriminates against interstate commerce; or (4) is not fairly related to the services provided by a state. In addition, in cases involving the taxation of foreign commerce, the Court examines (5) whether there is an "enhanced risk of multiple taxation," and (6) whether a state's tax interferes with the federal government's capacity to "speak with one voice when regulating commercial relations with foreign governments." Justice Ginsburg found California's "worldwide combined reporting" method of taxation to survive all but the third criteria. However, the justice concluded that Barclays had failed to show that the state's method of taxation in fact operated to impose an inordinate burden on multinational corporations. Justice O'Connor, joined by Justice Thomas, dissented.

THE DEVELOPMENT OF LAW

Rulings on State Regulatory Powers in Alleged Conflict with Federal Legislation

Case	Vote	Ruling
Northwest Airlines, Inc. v. County of Kent, Michigan, 114 S.Ct. 855 (1994)	7:1	Rebuffed a challenge to an airport system of collecting fees based on charging commercial airlines 100 percent of their square footage allocation costs, but only 20 percent of the same costs incurred by general aviation. Writing for the majority, Justice Ginsburg held that that system did not violate the Anti-Head Tax Act or burden interstate commerce. Justice Thomas dissented.
Livades v. Bradshaw, 114 S.Ct. – (1994)	9:0	Writing for the Court, Justice Souter held that a collective-bargain agreement was preempted under provisions of the National Labor Relations Act.

8

REPRESENTATIVE GOVERNMENT, VOTING RIGHTS, AND ELECTORAL POLITICS

B. VOTING RIGHTS AND THE REAPPORTIONMENT REVOLUTION

In *Shaw v. Reno*, 113 S.Ct. 2816 (1993) (see Vol. 1, Ch. 8), a bare majority of the Rehnquist Court ruled that the Fourteenth Amendment forbids racial gerrymandering in electoral redistricting unless the government demonstrates a "compelling reason" for creating so-called minority-majority districts. Justice O'Connor's opinion for the majority was so sweeping that it called into question the permissibility of race-conscious redistricting. But, on the last day of the 1993-1994 term, in two rulings on the Voting Rights Act, a majority of the Court took a different course and badly fragmented the Court, as well as drew an angry and lengthy opinion from Justice Thomas, who was joined by Justice Scalia.

In *Johnson v. De Grandy*, 114 S.Ct. – (1994), the Court overruled a court-ordered redistricting plan for Florida's House of Representatives. The plan would have increased the number of Hispanic-majority voting districts from nine to eleven out of a total of twenty districts. Writing for the Court, Justice Souter held that such minority-majority districts are permissible under the Voting Rights Act and sometimes necessary in order to increase minorities' representation, but ruled that the act does not require creating the greatest possible number of minority-majority districts. Once a minority group has achieved representation in "rough proportion" to its population, said Justice Souter, the Voting Rights Act requires nothing more. In this case, he concluded: "Treating equal political opportunity as the focus of the inquiry, we do not see how these district lines, apparently providing political effectiveness in proportion to voting-age numbers, deny equal political opportunity." Notably, Justice Souter avoided ruling on such related issues as how to measure the size of minority groups, whether as part of the overall population, the voting-age population, or the number of citizens eligible to vote. Specifying a "magic parameter," claimed the justice, was not necessary here. His opinion was joined by the chief justice and Justices Blackmun, Stevens, O'Connor, and Ginsburg, while Justice Kennedy joined only in part. Justices Scalia and Thomas dissented for reasons set forth more fully in their opinion in *Holder v. Hall.*

In the second case, *Holder v. Hall*, 114 S.Ct. – (1994), the Court not only split five to four, but the bare majority splintered three ways in different opinions. The result, nonetheless, was a reversal of an appellate court's decision ordering the change from a single-member county commission to a five-member commission with districts drawn so that at least one black commissioner could be elected. The case had originally been brought by black voters under Section 2 of the Voting Rights Act, which forbids any voting practice that denies or abridges the right to vote on the basis of race. They challenged the permissibility of the single-member commission in rural Bleckley, Georgia, where 20 percent of the county's population is black but where a black commissioner has never been elected.

With only Chief Justice Rehnquist and Justice O'Connor joining his opinion announcing the Court's decision in *Holder v. Hall,* Justice Kennedy rejected the claim that the Voting Rights Act permits challenges to the size of a governmental body or organization. He did so upon concluding that it was impossible to determine what size or structure would be best. Justice Kennedy's plurality opinion emphasized, for instance, that California has an 80-member assembly, while New Hampshire has 400 members in its House of Representatives. In a concurring opinion, Justice O'Connor further explained that there was no "limiting principle" for courts to insist on one size or another for a governing body. The result reached by these three justices was joined by concurring Justices Scalia and Thomas, though for different reasons and in order to form a bare majority for the outcome. They agreed with the result, but because they would have held that the Voting Rights Act does not govern race-conscious districting in the first place.

The four dissenters in *Holder v. Hall* countered that it was "clear" from the history of Bleckley county that the single-member commission had the effect of diluting the voting power of blacks. Justices Ginsburg, Stevens, and Souter joined Justice Blackmun's dissenting opinion. They maintained that the Voting Rights Act should remain available for attacking "subtler, more complex means of infringing minority voting strength," in cases such as here. In another opinion also joined by the three other dissenters, Justice Stevens rebutted what he termed the "radical reinterpretation" of the Voting Rights Act advanced by Justices Scalia and Thomas.

With Justice Scalia joining him in a fifty-nine page concurring opinion in *Holder v. Hall,* Justice Thomas expressly rejected over two decades of the Court's jurisprudence in the area of voting rights. The concept of minority-vote dilution has been central to the Court's analysis and interpretation of the Voting Rights Act. Yet, Thomas dismissed it as "a disastrous misadventure in judicial policymaking." "Our current practice should not continue," he claimed, "not for another term, not until the next case, not for another day." Instead, Thomas proposed that the Voting Rights Act should be reinterpreted to allow challenges solely to classical and overtly racially discriminatory practices bearing on voter qualifications. The Court's decision in *Allen v. State Board of Elections*, 393 U.S. 544 (1969), and other cases rejecting such a narrow reading of the Voting Rights Act, Thomas said, should simply be overturned and abandoned. The Court's approach to voting rights under the Voting Rights Act and the Fourteenth Amendment, in Thomas's words, had "given credence to the view that race defines political interest" and "should be repugnant to any nation that strives for the ideal of a color-blind Constitution."

C. CAMPAIGNS AND ELECTIONS

In its 1994-1995 term, the Court will review Ohio's requirement that campaign leaflets identify the individuals or organizations who prepare them in *McIntyre v. Ohio Elections Commission.* Margaret McIntyre was fined $100 for passing out leaflets opposing a tax referendum. The state supreme court upheld the fine and the disclosure requirement as a "minor burden" designed to identify "those responsible for fraud, false advertising and libel," rather than as an inhibition on political speech. But, McIntyre's attorneys contended that the statute was too broad and violated political rights "at the core of the electoral process." By contrast, the state attorney general, who had asked the Court to deny review, maintained that the statute was designed to preserve the integrity of the electoral process.

VOLUME TWO

3

ECONOMIC RIGHTS AND AMERICAN CAPITALISM

C. THE "TAKINGS CLAUSE" AND JUST COMPENSATION

Since the mid-1980s the Rehnquist Court has periodically revisited challenges to environmental, recreational, and other kinds of land-use regulations. Business groups and conservative organizations have pressed for an expansive reading of the Fifth Amendment's guarantee that "private property [shall not] be taken for public use, without just compensation." The "takings clause," however, has yet to be so expansively read by the Court as to threaten most land-use legislation. Within the Court, Justice Scalia has championed the broadest reading of the clause, but proven unable to command a majority for going very far in applying the clause as a limitation on governmental regulation. The most important and widely watched case, *Lucas v. South Carolina Coastal Council*, 112 S.Ct. 2886 (1992) (in Vol. 2, Ch. 3), raised a challenge to South Carolina's law forbidding the rebuilding of homes on beachfront property after Hurricane Hugo struck its coastline. Writing for the Court, Justice Scalia was only able to win agreement that in order to trigger the takings clause, regulations must deprive property owners of the entire economic value of their property. Since the vast majority of regulations do not deprive owners of 100 percent of their property's value, *Lucas* was a hollow victory for those seeking an expansive use of the taking clause.

Despite the ruling in *Lucas*, the Rehnquist Court once again revisited the issue in its 1993-1994 term in *Dolan v. City of Tigard*, 114 S.Ct. — (1994). That case presented a takings-clause challenge to city officials of Tigard, Oregon, who, as a condition for granting a building permit, required a storeowner to dedicate part of the property to public use. Specifically, Dolan was required to set aside about one-tenth of her 1.7 acre property as a public green, storm drainage channel, and path for bicyclers and pedestrians.

In *Dolan*, the Court split five to four in holding that the city had inadequately justified its requirements for a flood plain and a pathway. Writing for a bare majority, Chief Justice Rehnquist held that when government makes such determinations affecting private property, it must show a "rough proportionality" between their land-use restrictions and the harm to be prevented. Notably, though, the chief justice reaffirmed that government may simply ban all development in flood plains and that "no precise mathematical calculation" was required to justify land-use restrictions. As a result of the ruling in *Dolan*, state and local governments must satisfy a two-prong test: first, they must show that their restrictions serve a "legitimate public purpose" and, second, when imposing their restrictions they must undertake "some sort of individualized determination" establishing a "rough proportionality" between the restrictions and the harms to be averted. In a sharply worded dissent, joined by Justices Ginsburg and Blackmun, Justice Stevens took strong exception to the majority's heightened review of and new requirements on land-use regulations. In a separate opinion, Justice Souter dissented as well.

In addition, the Rehnquist Court confronted for the fourth time in the last five years a business's challenge to large punitive damage awards by juries under the due process clause, see *Honda Motor Co. v. Oberg*, 114 S.Ct. — (1994), in the next chapter.

Dolan v. City of Tigard

114 S.Ct. — (1994)

Florence Dolan applied to the city planning commission for approval to expand her store and pave her parking lot. Under a state comprehensive land management program, the commission held that her permit was conditioned on her dedicating part of her property to (1) a public greenway along Fanno Creek to minimize flooding that would be exacerbated by the increases in impervious surfaces associated with her development and (2) a pedestrian/bicycle pathway intended to relieve traffic congestion in the central business district of Tigard. Dolan objected and appealed the commission's denial of her request for variances from those requirements to the Land Use Board of Appeals (LUBA). She argued that the requirements were not related to the proposed development and therefore constituted an uncompensated taking of her property under the Fifth Amendment. The board, however, found a reasonable relationship between her proposed development and the requirement to dedicate land for a greenway, since the larger building and paved lot would increase the impervious surfaces and thus the runoff into the creek, and alleviating the impact of increased traffic from the development by providing a pathway as an alternative means of transportation. Both a state appellate court and the Oregon state supreme court affirmed the board's ruling and Dolan appealed to the Supreme Court.

The Court's decision was five to four. Chief Justice Rehnquist announced the majority's opinion, which Justices O'Connor, Kennedy, Scalia, and Thomas joined. Justice Stevens filed a dissenting opinion joined by Justices Ginsburg and Blackmun. Justice Souter dissented in a separate opinion.

Chief Justice REHNQUIST delivered the opinion of the Court.

We granted *certiorari* to resolve a question left open by our decision in *Nollan v. California Coastal Comm'n*, 483 U. S. 825 (1987), of what is the required degree of connection between the exactions imposed by the city and the projected impacts of the proposed development. . . .

The Commission made a series of findings concerning the relationship between the dedicated conditions and the projected impacts of petitioner's project. First, the Commission noted that "it is reasonable to assume that customers and employees of the future uses of this site could utilize a pedestrian/bicycle pathway adjacent to this development for their transportation and recreational needs." The Commission noted that the site plan has provided for bicycle parking in a rack in front of the proposed building and "it is reasonable to expect that some of the users of the bicycle parking provided for by the site plan will use the pathway adjacent to Fanno Creek if it is constructed." In addition, the Commission found that creation of a convenient, safe pedestrian/bicycle pathway system as an alternative means of transportation "could offset some of the traffic demand on [nearby] streets and lessen the increase in traffic congestion." . . .

Petitioner appealed to the Land Use Board of Appeals (LUBA) on the ground that the city's dedication requirements were not related to the proposed development, and, therefore, those requirements constituted an uncompensated taking of their property under the Fifth Amendment. . . .

The Takings Clause of the Fifth Amendment of the United States Constitution, made applicable to the States through the Fourteenth Amendment, *Chicago, B. & Q. R. Co. v. Chicago*, 166 U. S. 226 (1897), provides: "Nor shall private property be taken for public use, without just compensation." One of the principal purposes of the Takings Clause is "to bar Government from forcing some people alone to bear public burdens which, in all fairness and justice, should be borne by the public as a whole." *Armstrong v. United States*, 364 U. S. 40 (1960). Without question, had the city simply required petitioner to dedicate a strip of land along Fanno Creek for public use, rather than conditioning the grant of her permit to redevelop her property on such a dedication, a taking would have occurred. Such public access would deprive petitioner of the right to exclude others, "one of the most essential sticks in the bundle of rights that are commonly characterized as property." *Kaiser Aetna v. United States*, 444 U. S. 164 (1979).

On the other side of the ledger, the authority of state and local governments to engage in land use planning has been sustained against constitutional challenge as long ago as our decision in *Euclid v. Ambler Realty Co.*, 272 U. S. 365 (1926). . . . The sort of land use regulations discussed in the cases just cited, however, differ in two relevant particulars from the present case. First, they involved essentially legislative determinations classifying entire areas of the city, whereas here the city made an adjudicative decision to condition petitioner's application for a building permit on an individual parcel. Second, the conditions imposed were not simply a limitation on the use petitioner might make of her own parcel, but a requirement that she deed portions of the property to the city. In *Nollan*, we held that governmental authority to exact such a condition was circumscribed by the Fifth and Fourteenth Amendments. Under the well-settled doctrine of "unconstitutional conditions," the government may not require a person to give up a constitutional right—here the right to receive just compensation when property is taken for a public use—in exchange for a discretionary benefit conferred by the government where the property sought has little or no relationship to the benefit. . . .

In evaluating petitioner's claim, we must first determine whether the "essential nexus" exists between the "legitimate state interest" and the permit condition exacted by the city. *Nollan*. If we find that a nexus exists, we must then decide the required degree of connection between the exactions and the projected impact of the proposed development. We were not required to reach this question in *Nollan*, because we concluded that the connection did not meet even the loosest standard. Here, however, we must decide this question. . . .

Undoubtedly, the prevention of flooding along Fanno Creek and the reduction of traffic congestion in the Central Business District qualify as the type of legitimate public purposes we have upheld. It seems equally obvious that a nexus exists between preventing flooding along Fanno Creek and limiting development within the creek's 100-year floodplain. Petitioner proposes to double the size of her retail store and to pave her now-gravel parking lot, thereby expanding the impervious surface on the property and increasing the amount of stormwater run-off into Fanno Creek. The same may be said for the city's attempt to reduce traffic congestion by providing for alternative means of transportation. . . .

The second part of our analysis requires us to determine whether the degree of the exactions demanded by the city's permit conditions bear the required relationship to the projected impact of petitioner's proposed development. Here the Oregon Supreme Court deferred to what it termed the "city's unchallenged factual findings" supporting the dedication conditions and found them to be reasonably related to the impact of the expansion of petitioner's business.

The city required that petitioner dedicate "to the city as Greenway all portions of the site that fall within the existing 100-year floodplain [of Fanno Creek] . . . and all property 15 feet above [the floodplain] boundary." In addition, the city demanded that the retail store be designed so as not to intrude into the greenway area. The city relies on the Commission's rather tentative findings that increased stormwater flow from petitioner's property "can only add to the public need to manage the [floodplain] for drainage purposes" to support its conclusion that the "requirement of dedication of the floodplain area on the site is related to the applicant's plan to intensify development on the site." . . .

The question for us is whether these findings are constitutionally sufficient to justify the conditions imposed by the city on petitioner's building permit. Since state courts have been dealing with this question a good deal longer than we have, we turn to representative decisions made by them. . . .

We think the "reasonable relationship" test adopted by a majority of the state courts is closer to the federal constitutional norm than either of those previously discussed. But we do not adopt it as such . . . . We think a term such as "rough proportionality" best encapsulates what we hold to be the requirement of the Fifth Amendment. No precise mathematical calculation is required, but the city must make some sort of individualized determination that the required dedication is related both in nature and extent to the impact of the proposed development. . . .

If petitioner's proposed development had somehow encroached on existing greenway space in the city, it would have been reasonable to require petitioner to provide some alternative greenway space for the public either on her property or elsewhere. But that is not the case here. We conclude that the findings upon which the city relies do not show the required reasonable relationship between the floodplain easement and the petitioner's proposed new building. With respect to the pedestrian/bicycle pathway, we have no doubt that the city was correct in finding that the larger retail sales facility proposed by petitioner will increase traffic on the streets of the Central Business District. The city estimates that the proposed development would generate roughly 435 additional trips per day. . . . But on the record before us, the city has not met its burden of demonstrating that the additional number of vehicle and bicycle trips generated by the petitioner's development reasonably relate to the city's requirement for a dedication of the pedestrian/bicycle pathway easement. The city simply found that the creation of the pathway "could offset some of the traffic demand . . . and lessen the increase in traffic congestion."

No precise mathematical calculation is required, but the city must make some effort to quantify its findings in support of the dedication for the pedestrian/bicycle pathway beyond the conclusory statement that it could offset some of the traffic demand generated. . . . The city's goals of reducing flooding hazards and traffic congestion, and providing for public greenways, are laudable, but there are outer limits to how this may be done.

Justice STEVENS, with whom Justice BLACKMUN and Justice GINSBURG join, dissenting.

The Court is correct in concluding that the city may not attach arbitrary conditions to a building permit or to a variance even when it can rightfully deny the application outright. I also agree that state court decisions dealing with ordinances that govern municipal development plans provide useful guidance in a case of this kind. Yet the Court's description of the doctrinal underpinnings of its decision, the phrasing of its fledgling test of "rough proportionality," and the application of that test to this case run contrary to the traditional treatment of these cases and break considerable and unpropitious new ground.

Candidly acknowledging the lack of federal precedent for its exercise in rulemaking, the Court purports to find guidance in 12 "representative" state court decisions. To do so is certainly appropriate. The state cases the Court consults, however, either fail to support or decidedly undermine the Court's conclusions in key respects. . . .

It is not merely state cases, but our own cases as well, that require the analysis to focus on the impact of the city's action on the entire parcel of private property. In *Penn Central Transportation Co. v. New York City*, 438 U. S. 104 (1978), we stated that takings jurisprudence "does not divide a single parcel into discrete segments and attempt to determine whether rights in a particular segment have been entirely abrogated." Instead, this Court focuses "both on the character of the action and on the nature and extent of the interference with rights in the parcel as a whole." *Andrus v. Allard*, 444 U. S. 51 (1979), reaffirmed the nondivisibility principle outlined in *Penn Central*, stating that "at least where an owner possesses a full 'bundle' of property rights, the destruction of one 'strand' of the bundle is not a taking, because the aggregate must be viewed in its entirety." . . .

The Court has made a serious error by abandoning the traditional presumption of constitutionality and imposing a novel burden of proof on a city implementing an admittedly valid comprehensive land use plan. Even more consequential than its incorrect disposition of this case, however, is the Court's resurrection of a species of substantive due process analysis that it firmly rejected decades ago.

The Court begins its constitutional analysis by citing *Chicago, B. & Q. R. Co. v. Chicago*, 166 U. S. 226 (1897), for the proposition that the Takings Clause of the Fifth Amendment is "applicable to the States through the Fourteenth Amendment." Ante, at 8. That opinion, however, contains no mention of either the Takings Clause or the Fifth Amendment; it held that the protection afforded by the Due Process Clause of the Fourteenth Amendment extends to matters of substance as well as procedure, and that the substance of "the due process of law enjoined by the Fourteenth Amendment requires compensation to be made or adequately secured to the owner of private property taken for public use under the authority of a State." *Chicago, B. & Q. R. Co.* It applied the same kind of substantive due process analysis more frequently identified with a better known case that accorded similar substantive protection to a baker's liberty interest in working 60 hours a week and 10 hours a day. See *Lochner v. New York*, 198 U. S. 45 (1905).

Later cases have interpreted the Fourteenth Amendment's substantive protection against uncompensated deprivations of private property by the

States as though it incorporated the text of the Fifth Amendment's Takings Clause. There was nothing problematic about that interpretation in cases enforcing the Fourteenth Amendment against state action that involved the actual physical invasion of private property. Justice HOLMES charted a significant new course, however, when he opined that a state law making it "commercially impracticable to mine certain coal" had "very nearly the same effect for constitutional purposes as appropriating or destroying it." *Pennsylvania Coal Co. v. Mahon*, 260 U. S. 393 (1922). The so-called "regulatory takings" doctrine that the HOLMES dictum kindled has an obvious kinship with the line of substantive due process cases that *Lochner* exemplified. Besides having similar ancestry, both doctrines are potentially open-ended sources of judicial power to invalidate state economic regulations that Members of this Court view as unwise or unfair.

This case inaugurates an even more recent judicial innovation than the regulatory takings doctrine: the application of the "unconstitutional conditions" label to a mutually beneficial transaction between a property owner and a city. The Court tells us that the city's refusal to grant Dolan a discretionary benefit infringes her right to receive just compensation for the property interests that she has refused to dedicate to the city "where the property sought has little or no relationship to the benefit." Although it is well settled that a government cannot deny a benefit on a basis that infringes constitutionally protected interests–"especially [one's] interest in freedom of speech," *Perry v. Sindermann*, 408 U. S. 593 (1972)–the "unconstitutional conditions" doctrine provides an inadequate framework in which to analyze this case.

Dolan has no right to be compensated for a taking unless the city acquires the property interests that she has refused to surrender. Since no taking has yet occurred, there has not been any infringement of her constitutional right to compensation. . . .

In its application of what is essentially the doctrine of substantive due process, the Court confuses the past with the present. On November 13, 1922, the village of Euclid, Ohio, adopted a zoning ordinance that effectively confiscated 75 percent of the value of property owned by the Ambler Realty Company. Despite its recognition that such an ordinance "would have been rejected as arbitrary and oppressive" at an earlier date, the Court (over the dissent of Justices VAN DEVANTER, MCREYNOLDS, and BUTLER) upheld the ordinance. Today's majority should heed the words of Justice SUTHERLAND:

> "Such regulations are sustained, under the complex conditions of our day, for reasons analogous to those which justify traffic regulations, which, before the advent of automobiles and rapid transit street railways, would have been condemned as fatally arbitrary and unreasonable. And in this there is no inconsistency, for while the meaning of constitutional guaranties never varies, the scope of their application must expand or contract to meet the new and different conditions which are constantly coming within the field of their operation. In a changing world, it is impossible that it should be otherwise." *Euclid v. Ambler Co.*, 272 U. S. 365 (1926).

In our changing world one thing is certain: uncertainty will characterize predictions about the impact of new urban developments on the risks of floods, earthquakes, traffic congestion, or environmental harms. When there is doubt concerning the magnitude of those impacts, the public interest in averting them must outweigh the private interest of the commercial entrepreneur. If the government can demonstrate that the conditions it has imposed in a land-use permit are rational, impartial and conducive to fulfilling the aims of a valid land-use plan, a strong presumption of validity should attach to those conditions. The burden of demonstrating that those conditions have unreasonably impaired the economic value of the proposed improvement belongs squarely on the shoulders of the party challenging the state action's constitutionality. That allocation of burdens has served us well in the past. The Court has stumbled badly today by reversing it.

4

THE NATIONALIZATION OF THE BILL OF RIGHTS

B. THE RISE AND RETREAT OF THE "DUE PROCESS REVOLUTION"

The Rehnquist Court has generally rebuffed attempts to have it read broadly the Fifth and Fourteenth Amendments' due process clauses, both in the direction of extending their procedural safeguards and in legitimating new substantive liberty interests. However, there have been a couple of exceptions. In *Foucha v. United States*, 112 S.Ct. 1780 (1992) (see Vol. 2, Ch. 4), a bare majority struck down Louisiana's law permitting the continued institutionalization of an individual who was criminally acquitted by reason of insanity and who subsequently regained sanity but was still deemed to pose a potential threat to society.

In 1993, then, another bare majority in *United States v. James Daniel Good Real Property*, 114 S.Ct. 492 (1993) (see below), held that convicted drug dealers must be given a hearing before the government seizes their property under forfeiture laws. Notably, the ruling in *James Daniel Good Real Property* was also the third time that a majority of the Rehnquist Court rejected the government's arguments for expansive powers to seize the property of convicted drug dealers as part of its "war on drugs." In *Alexander v. United States*, 113 S.Ct. 2766 (1993), and *Austin v. United States*, 113 S.Ct. 2801 (1993) (see Vol. 2, Ch. 9), the Court held that such seizures are subject to the limitations of the Eighth Amendment's bar against "excessive fines," which prevents the government from going after huge real estate parcels for comparatively small offenses.

For the fourth time in five years the Court also granted a case attacking large punitive damage awards as a denial of substantive and procedural due process. In *Pacific Mutual Life Insurance Company v. Haslip*, 499 U.S. 1 (1991), voting eight to one, the justices rejected such a challenge. Dissenting Justice O'Connor was the only one willing to thrust the Court into this area of litigation and to expand judicial review over common law jury awards. When last term the Court for the third time rejected a due process challenge to another large punitive damage award, in *TXO Production Corp. v. Alliance Resources Corp.*, 113 S.Ct. 2711 (1993) (in Vol. 2, Ch. 4), however, Justice O'Connor's dissent was joined by two others, Justices Souter and White.

In its 1993-1994 term the Rehnquist Court again took up the matter of large damage awards in *Honda Motor Co. v. Oberg*, 114 S.Ct. — (1994). There, the Court reviewed a due process challenge to Oregon's law barring trial and appellate court judges from questioning juries about the size of their punitive damage awards. Oregon's law, which is the only one of its kind, barred judicial review of jury awards "unless the court can affirmatively say there is no evidence to support the verdict." The case stemmed from an accident on an all-terrain vehicle manufactured by Honda and a subsequent personal injury lawsuit in which a jury awarded over five million dollars in punitive damages. Attorneys for Honda appealed that award on the ground the due process clause should limit excessive punitive damage awards.

By a vote of seven to two, the Court struck down Oregon's limitation on judicial review of jury awards as a violation of due process. Writing for the majority, Justice Stevens wrote broadly about guarding against excessive punitive damage awards. "Punitive damages pose an acute danger of arbitrary deprivation of property," he said, adding that there are constitutional limitations on punitive damage awards, on those that are "grossly excessive." But, as in prior rulings, Justice Stevens stopped short of indicating what those limitations are or how to draw them. In a concurring opinion, Justice Scalia emphasized that this was a procedural due process case. Justice Ginsburg, joined by Chief Justice Rehnquist, dissented and argued that Oregon's procedures for instructing juries on awarding punitive damages were constitutionally adequate.

In two companion cases, *Victor v. Nebraska* and *Sandoval v. California*, 114 S.Ct. 1239 (1994), the Court also revisited the issue of the adequacy of jury instructions for determining whether the accused is guilty "beyond a reasonable doubt." Both cases represented due process challenges to jury instructions that included references to "moral certainty" about the defendant's guilt. In the California case, the jury in a capital case was told that,

> Reasonable doubt is defined as follows: It is not a mere possible doubt; because everything relating to human affairs, and depending on moral evidence, is open to some possible or imaginary doubt. It is that state of the case which, after the entire comparison and consideration of all the evidence, leaves the minds of the jurors in that condition that they cannot say they feel an abiding conviction, to a moral certainty, of the truth of the charge.

Writing for a unanimous Court in *Sandoval*, Justice O'Connor rejected the due process challenge to that jury instruction and held that within its context the reference to "moral certainty" was neither vague nor unconstitutional, though the justice added that "we do not condone" the use of the phrase. In *Victor v. Nebraska*, Justice O'Connor upheld as well jury instructions that include, along with a reference to "moral certainty," the jury's finding the "accused guilty upon the strong probablities of the case, provided such probabilities are strong enough to exclude any doubt of his guilt that is reasonable." However, dissenting in that case, Justices Blackmun and Souter contended that the instructions were too vague and might be construed by juries to mean that "a large as opposed to a merely reasonable doubt is required to acquit a defendant."

United States v. James Daniel Good Real Property

114 S.Ct. 492 (1993)

Almost five years after police found drugs in James Daniel Good's home and he pleaded guilty to violating Hawaii's drug laws, the federal government sought the forfeiture of his house and land under federal law. The government did so on the ground that his property had been used in the commission of a federal drug offense. Following an *ex parte* proceeding (at which Good was not present), a federal magistrate issued a warrant authorizing the seizure of Good's property's. Subsequently, without prior notice or an adversary proceeding, the government seized Good's property. Good challenged the government's actions, arguing that he was deprived of his property without due process of law.

The Court's decision was five to four. Justice Kennedy announced the majority's opinion, which Justices Blackmun, Stevens, Souter, and Ginsburg joined. Chief Justice Rehnquist filed an opinion in part concurring and dissenting, which Justices O'Connor and Scalia joined. Separate opinions concurring and dissenting in part were also filed by Justices O'Connor and Thomas.

Justice KENNEDY delivered the opinion of the Court.

The Due Process Clause of the Fifth Amendment guarantees that "no person shall . . . be deprived of life, liberty, or property, without due process of law." Our precedents establish the general rule that individuals must receive notice and an opportunity to be heard before the Government deprives them of property.

The Government does not, and could not, dispute that the seizure of Good's home and four-acre parcel deprived him of property interests protected by the Due Process Clause. By the Government's own submission, the seizure gave it the right to charge rent, to condition occupancy, and even to evict the occupants. Instead, the Government argues that it afforded Good all the process the Constitution requires. The Government makes two separate points in this regard. First, it contends that compliance with the Fourth Amendment suffices when the Government seizes property for purposes of forfeiture. In the alternative, it argues that the seizure of real property under the drug forfeiture laws justifies an exception to the usual due process requirement of preseizure notice and hearing. . . .

Though the Fourth Amendment places limits on the Government's power to seize property for purposes of forfeiture, it does not provide the sole measure of constitutional protection that must be afforded property owners in forfeiture proceedings. So even assuming that the Fourth Amendment were satisfied in this case, it remains for us to determine whether the seizure complied with our well-settled jurisprudence under the Due Process Clause.

Whether *ex parte* seizures of forfeitable property satisfy the Due Process Clause is a question we last confronted in *Calero-Toledo v. Pearson Yacht Leasing Co.*, 416 U.S. 663 (1974), which held that the Government could seize a yacht subject to civil forfeiture without affording prior notice or hearing. Central to our analysis in *Calero-Toledo* was the fact that a yacht was the "sort [of property] that could be removed to another jurisdiction, destroyed, or concealed, if advance warning of confiscation were given." The ease with which an owner could frustrate the Government's interests in the forfeitable property created a "'special need for very prompt action'" that justified the postponement of notice and hearing until after the seizure.

We had no occasion in *Calero-Toledo* to decide whether the same considerations apply to the forfeiture of real property, which, by its very nature, can be neither moved nor concealed. In fact, when *Calero-Toledo* was decided, both the Puerto Rican statute, and the federal forfeiture statute upon which it was modeled authorized the forfeiture of personal property only. It was not until 1984, ten years later, that Congress amended [federal law] to authorize the forfeiture of real property.

The right to prior notice and a hearing is central to the Constitution's command of due process. . . . We tolerate some exceptions to the general rule requiring predeprivation notice and hearing, but only in "'extraordinary situations where some valid governmental interest is at stake that justifies postponing the hearing until after the event.'" Whether the seizure of real property for purposes of civil forfeiture justifies such an exception requires an examination of the competing interests at stake, along with the promptness and adequacy of later proceedings. The three-part inquiry set forth in *Mathews v. Eldridge*, 424 U.S. 319 (1976), provides guidance in this regard. The *Mathews* analysis requires us to consider the private interest affected by the official action; the risk of an erroneous deprivation of that interest through the procedures used, as well as the probable value of additional safeguards; and the Government's interest, including the administrative burden that additional procedural requirements would impose.

Good's right to maintain control over his home, and to be free from governmental interference, is a private interest of historic and continuing importance. The seizure deprived Good of valuable rights of ownership, including the right of sale, the right of occupancy, the right to unrestricted use and enjoyment, and the right to receive rents. All that the seizure left him, by the Government's own submission, was the right to bring a claim for the return of title at some unscheduled future hearing. . . .

The purpose of an adversary hearing is to ensure the requisite neutrality that must inform all governmental decisionmaking. That protection is of particular importance here, where the Government has a direct pecuniary interest in the outcome of the proceeding. Moreover, the availability of a postseizure hearing may be no recompense for losses caused by erroneous seizure. Given the congested civil dockets in federal courts, a claimant may not receive an adversary hearing until many months after the seizure. And even if the ultimate judicial decision is that the claimant was an innocent owner, or that the Government lacked probable cause, this determination, coming months after the seizure, "would not cure the temporary deprivation that an earlier hearing might have prevented."

This brings us to the third consideration under *Mathews*, "the Government's interest, including the function involved and the fiscal and administrative burdens that the additional or substitute procedural requirement would entail." The governmental interest we consider here is not some general interest in forfeiting property but the specific interest in seizing real property before the forfeiture hearing. The question in the civil forfeiture context is whether ex parte seizure is justified by a pressing need for prompt action. We find no pressing need here.

In the usual case, the Government thus has various means, short of seizure, to protect its legitimate interests in forfeitable real property. There is no reason to take the additional step of asserting control over the property without first affording notice and an adversary hearing.

Requiring the Government to postpone seizure until after an adversary hearing creates no significant administrative burden. A claimant is already entitled to an adversary hearing before a final judgment of forfeiture. No extra hearing would be required in the typical case, since the Government can wait until after the forfeiture judgment to seize the property. From an administrative standpoint it makes little difference whether that hearing is held before or after the seizure. And any harm that results from delay is minimal in comparison to the injury occasioned by erroneous seizure. . . .

Chief Justice REHNQUIST, with whom Justices SCALIA and O'CONNOR join, concurring in part and dissenting in part.

The Court applies the three-factor balancing test for evaluating procedural due process claims set out in *Mathews v. Eldridge*, 424 U.S. 319 (1976), to reach its unprecedented holding. I reject the majority's expansive application of *Mathews*. . . .

The Court's fixation on *Mathews* sharply conflicts with both historical practice and the specific textual source of the Fourth Amendment's "reasonableness" inquiry. The Fourth Amendment strikes a balance between the people's security in their persons, houses, papers, and effects and the public interest in effecting searches and seizures for law enforcement purposes. Compliance with the standards and procedures prescribed by the Fourth Amendment constitutes all the "process" that is "due" to respondent Good under the Fifth Amendment in the forfeiture context. . . .

Justice O'CONNOR, concurring in part and dissenting in part.

My first disagreement is with the Court's holding that the Government must give notice and a hearing before seizing any real property prior to forfeiting it. That conclusion is inconsistent with over a hundred years of our case law. We have already held that seizure for purpose of forfeiture is one of those "extraordinary situations," *Fuentes v. Shevin*, 407 U.S. 67 (1972), in which the Due Process Clause does not require predeprivation notice and an opportunity to be heard. *Calero-Toledo v. Pearson Yacht Leasing Co.*, 416 U.S. 663 (1974). As we have recognized, *Calero-Toledo* "clearly indicates that due process does not require federal [agents] to conduct a hearing before seizing items subject to forfeiture." . . . [T]he property owner receives all the process that is due at the forfeiture hearing itself.

The distinction the Court tries to draw between our precedents and this case—the only distinction it can draw—is that real property is somehow different than personal property for due process purposes. But that distinction has never been considered constitutionally relevant in our forfeiture cases. . . .

My second disagreement is with the Court's holding that the Government acted unconstitutionally in seizing this real property for forfeiture without giving Good prior notice and an opportunity to be heard. I agree that the due process inquiry outlined in *Mathews v. Eldridge*, 424 U.S. 319 (1976)—which requires a consideration of the private interest affected, the risk of erroneous deprivation and the value of additional safeguards, and the Government's interest—provides an appropriate analytical framework for evaluating whether a governmental practice violates the Due Process Clause notwithstanding its historical pedigree. But this case is an as applied challenge to the seizure of Good's property; on these facts, I cannot conclude that there was a constitutional violation. . . .

Finally, the burden on the Government of the Court's decision will be substantial. The practical effect of requiring an adversary hearing before seizure will be that the Government will conduct the full forfeiture hearing on the merits before it can claim its interest in the property. In the meantime, the Government can protect the important federal interests at stake only through the vagaries of state laws. And while under the current system only a few property owners contest the forfeiture, the Court's opinion creates an incentive and an opportunity to do so, thus increasing the workload of federal prosecutors and courts. . . .

THE DEVELOPMENT OF LAW

Rulings on Substantive and Procedural Due Process

Case	Vote	Ruling
Weiss v. United States, 114 S.Ct. 752 (1994)	9:0	Unanimously rejected a due process challenge to the way military judges in courts martial are appointed and given fixed tenures.
Albright v. Oliver, 114 S.Ct. 807 (1994)	7:2	Rejected a substantive due process claim that the initiation of a baseless criminal prosecution, based on perjured testimony that the accused was selling drugs when the alleged drug was in fact baking soda, provides a basis for a constitutional tort action against state officials. Justices Stevens and Blackmun dissented.
United States v. Carlton, 114 S.Ct. — (1994)	9:0	Held that Congress's retroactive application of a 1987 amendment to the Internal Revenue Service Code, pertaining to estate tax deductions, had a rational basis and did not violate due process.
Honda Motor Co. v. Oberg, 114 S.Ct. – (1994)	7:2	Writing for the Court, Justice Stevens held that due process requires that jury awards of punitive damages be reviewable by courts. Justice Ginsburg and Chief Justice Rehnquist dissented.

5

FREEDOM OF EXPRESSION AND ASSOCIATION

A. JUDICIAL APPROACHES TO THE FIRST AMENDMENT

In its 1994-1995 term the Court will consider a First Amendment challenge to a controversial ban on federal employees' receiving honoraria for giving speeches and publishing articles and books. In *United States v. National Treasury Employees Union*, the federal government appealed an appellate court's holding that the ban, imposed under the Ethics Reform Act of 1989, violates federal workers' free speech rights under the First Amendment.

In another decision bearing on the First Amendment rights of public workers, in *Waters v. Churchill*, 114 S.Ct. — (1994), the Court, on the one hand, reaffirmed the broad power of federal, state, and local governments to restrict their employees' speech. But, on the other hand, the Court ruled for the first time that the First Amendment confers a procedural guarantee requiring employers to conduct some kind of investigation into the basis for disciplining or firing employees for speech deemed to be subordinate. Cheryl Churchill was fired from her position as a nurse in a city hospital after administrators were told by other nurses that she had criticized the obstetrics department and denigrated her supervisors, while Churchill claimed that she was simply raising concerns about patient care and staff shortages.

Writing for the majority in *Waters*, Justice O'Connor reaffirmed that "the extra power the government has in this area comes from the nature of the government's mission as an employer. When someone who is paid a salary so that she will contribute to an agency's effective operation begins to do or say things that detract from the agency's effective operation, the government employer must have some power to restrain her." Only dissenting Justices Blackmun and Stevens thought otherwise. They charged the Court's majority with "underestimat[ing] the importance of freedom of speech for the more than 18 million civilian employees of this country's federal, state, and local governments, and subordinat[ing] that freedom to an abstract interest in bureaucratic efficiency."

Justice O'Connor's opinion for the Court, however, proceeded to hold that government employers disciplining or firing employees for their speech "must tread with a certain amount of care" and conduct an investigation into the basis for their action. The First Amendment, O'Connor ruled, contains a procedural safeguard against the erroneous punishment of protected speech, though that safeguard depends on each case and consideration of its costs versus the risks posed for employees' free speech. No specific kind of investigation must be conducted or is constitutionally required, the justice concluded, when declining to lay down further guidelines. "Many different courses of action will necessarily be reasonable," O'Connor added, depending on a case-by-case analysis. In so holding, Justice O'Connor picked up the votes of Justices Blackmun and Stevens but lost those of Justices Scalia, Kennedy, and Thomas. In a separate opinion joined by the latter justices, Scalia countered that the First Amendment imposed no such procedural requirement and sharply attacked O'Connor's analysis as unprecedented, ambiguious, and certain to burden government employers and the courts.

D. COMMERCIAL SPEECH

While not reaching the issue of the First Amendment's protection in *Campbell aka Luke Skywalker v. Acuff-Rose Music, Inc.*, 114 S.Ct. 1164 (1994), the Court ruled that commercial parodies are permissible under federal copyright law. Under federal copyright law, the sole exception to a copyright owner's exclusive right to control their works is the doctrine of "fair use." In an important ruling, the Court reversed an appellate court's decision that 2 Live Crew's "blatantly commercial purpose" in recording a parody of Roy Orbison's 1964 rock song "Oh, Pretty Woman" violated federal copyright law. In 2 Live Crew's version of Orbinson's rock classic, the "pretty woman" of the first verse becomes "big hairy woman," "bald headed woman," and "two timin' woman."

Writing for a unanimous Court, Justice David Souter held that parody was entitled to consideration, like other kinds of commentaries, as a fair use of copyrighted materials. Under the fair use doctrine, portions of a copyrighted work may be used without permission "for purposes such as criticism, comment, news reporting, teaching, scholarship or research." The rap group's parody, in Justice Souter's words, "can be taken as a comment on the naivete of the original of an earlier day, as a rejections of its sentiment that ignores the ugliness of street life and the debasement that it signifies." The humor of parody, he observed, "necessarily springs from recognizable allusion to its object through distorted imitation." Because a parody's "art lies in the tension between a known original and its parodic twin," a parody has to use enough of the original to be recognizable to the audience. As a result, courts must decide on a case-by-case basis whether a parody qualifies as a fair use exception to federal copyright law.

In two other rulings handed down during its 1993-1994 term, the Court dealt with issues arising from the application of its commercial speech doctrine. *Ibanez v. Florida Department of Professional Regulation, Board of Accountancy*, 114 S.Ct. — (1994) involved a First Amendment challenge to Florida's ban on the use of the appellations CPA (certified public accountant) and CFP (certified financial planner) on business cards, letterheads, and in telephone listings. By a vote of seven to two, the justices continued a two-decade-old trend towards according commercial speech greater First Amendment protection. Writing for the majority, Justice Ginsburg reaffirmed that states may "ban such speech only if it is false, deceptive, or misleading." Restrictions on such advertising must "directly and materially advance a substantial state interest in a manner no more extensive than necessary to serve [the state's] interest." Here, the Court's majority rejected Florida's claim that the use of "certified CPA" in advertisements was "inherently misleading" as insubstantial and outweighed by the First Amendment. By contrast, dissenting Justice O'Connor, along with Chief Justice Rehnquist, contended that, "States may prohibit inherently misleading speech entirely."

In *City of Ladue v. Gilleo*, 114 S.Ct. — (1994), the Court heard an appeal of a federal appellate court's striking down of a municipal ordinance banning the posting of all signs, except for real estate sale signs, on private property. Since its founding in 1936, Ladue, Missouri, banned all signs, with the exception of "For Sale" signs, in order to preserve the city's "unique aesthetic character." But, in December 1990, shortly after the United States' clash with Iraq, an anti-war protester, Margaret Gilleo, ran afoul of the ordinance by placing an 8 1/2-by-11-inch sign, "For Peace in Gulf," in a second-floor window of her home after two other similar signs she posted on her front lawn disappeared mysteriously. Gilleo in turn challenged the constitutionality of Ladue's ordinance in court and won, whereupon the city appealed to the Supreme Court.

When announcing the Court's decision in *City of Ladue*, Justice Stevens struck down the city's ordinance in a sweeping opinion that went beyond the lower courts' analysis rejecting Ladue's justification for its ban on noncommercial signs. The lower courts had held that Ladue's ordinance was flawed in giving favored status to commercial, as opposed to political, speech and was thus underinclusive. By contrast, Justice Stevens took the position that the ordinance was overinclusive and too restrictive. In his words:

> Ladue has almost completely foreclosed a venerable means of communication that is both unique and important. It has totally foreclosed that medium to political, religious, or personal messages. Signs that react to a local happening or express a view on a controversial issue both reflect and animate change in the life of a community. Often placed on lawns or in windows, residential signs play an important part in political campaigns, during which they are displayed to signal the resident's support for particular candidates, parties, or causes. They may not afford the same opportunities for conveying complex ideas as do other media, but residential signs have long been an important and distinct medium of expression. . . .

Residential signs are an unusually cheap and convenient form of communication. Especially for persons of modest means or limited mobility, a yard or window sign may have no practical substitute. Even for the affluent, the added costs in money or time of taking out a newspaper advertisement, handing out leaflets on the street, or standing in front of one's house with a hand-held sign may make the difference between participating and not participating in some public debate. Furthermore, a person who puts up a sign at her residence often intends to reach neighbors, an audience that could not be reached nearly as well by other means.

A special respect for individual liberty in the home has long been part of our culture and our law; that principle has special resonance when the government seeks to constrain a person's ability to speak there. Most Americans would be understandably dismayed, given that tradition, to learn that it was illegal to display from their window an 8-by-11-inch sign expressing their political views. Whereas the government's need to mediate among various competing uses, including expressive ones, for public streets and facilities is constant and unavoidable, its need to regulate temperate speech from the home is surely much less pressing.

Our decision that Ladue's ban on almost all residential signs violates the First Amendment by no means leaves the City powerless to address the ills that may be associated with residential signs. It bears mentioning that individual residents themselves have strong incentives to keep their own property values up and to prevent "visual clutter" in their own yards and neighborhoods–incentives markedly different from those of persons who erect signs on others' land, in others' neighborhoods, or on public property. Residents' self-interest diminishes the danger of the "unlimited" proliferation of residential signs that concerns the City of Ladue. We are confident that more temperate measures could in large part satisfy Ladue's stated regulatory needs without harm to the First Amendment rights of its citizens. As currently framed, however, the ordinance abridges those rights.

F. REGULATING THE BROADCAST AND CABLE MEDIA

In 1992, Congress overrode a presidential veto to enact the Cable Television Consumer Protection and Competition Act. That legislation subjects the cable industry to rate regulation by the Federal Communications Commission (FCC) and by municipal franchising authorities; prohibits municipalities from awarding exclusive franchises to cable operators; imposes various restrictions on cable programmers that are affiliated with cable operators; and directs the FCC to develop and promulgate regulations imposing minimum technical standards for cable operators. In *Turner Broadcasting System, Inc. v. Federal Communications Commission*, 114 S.Ct. — (1994), the constitutionality of two "must-carry provisions" was challenged as a violation of the First Amendment. Section 4 of the act requires cable companies to carry "local commercial television stations," other than those qualifying as "noncommercial educational" stations under Section 5, that operate within the same television market as the cable system. Cable systems with more than twelve active channels, and more than three hundred subscribers, are required to set aside up to one-third of their channels for commercial broadcast stations that request carriage. Cable systems with more than three hundred subscribers, but only twelve or fewer active channels, must carry the signals of three commercial broadcast stations. Section 5 of the act imposes similar requirements regarding the carriage of local public broadcast television stations.

Attorneys for the cable industry argued that the regulations effectively dictated what kinds of programs are carried and wrongly favored local broadcasters over other programers or speakers. As a result of the "must-carry" regulations some cable systems dropped C-SPAN, for instance, in favor of local broadcasters. By contrast, lawyers for the FCC defended the regulations as within Congress's power to protect local broadcasters' ability to compete for viewing audiences and advertising.

Writing for the Court, Justice Kennedy held for the first time that the First Amendment extends protection to the cable industry and requires heightened judicial review of any regulations or restrictions in light of the differences between broadcast and cable technologies. On that issue the justices were unanimous. But Justice Kennedy commanded only four other votes—those of the chief justice and Justices Stevens, Blackmun, and Souter—on the central issue of the constitutionality of the "must-carry" provisions. On that issue a bare majority declined to strike down the regulations and remanded the case back to the lower court for re-consideration of the basis for the regulations. In Justice Kennedy's words:

> [T]he must-carry provisions are not designed to favor or disadvantage speech of any particular content. Rather, they are meant to protect broadcast television from what Congress determined to be unfair competition by cable systems. In enacting the provisions, Congress sought to preserve the existing structure of the Nation's broadcast television medium while permitting the concomitant expansion and development of cable television, and, in particular, to ensure that broadcast television remains available as a source of video programming for those without cable. Appellants' ability to hypothesize a content-based purpose for these provisions rests on little more than speculation and does not cast doubt upon the content-neutral character of must-carry. Indeed, "it is a familiar principle of constitutional law that this Court will not strike down an otherwise constitutional statute on the basis of an alleged illicit legislative motive." *United States v. O'Brien*, 391 U. S. 367 (1968) (citing *McCray v. United States*, 195 U. S. 27 (1904)). . . .
>
> Under *O'Brien*, a content-neutral regulation will be sustained if "it furthers an important or substantial governmental interest; if the governmental interest is unrelated to the suppression of free expression; and if the inciden-

tal restriction on alleged First Amendment freedoms is no greater than is essential to the furtherance of that interest." To satisfy this standard, a regulation need not be the least speech-restrictive means of advancing the Government's interests. "Rather, the requirement of narrow tailoring is satisfied 'so long as the . . . regulation promotes a substantial government interest that would be achieved less effectively absent the regulation.'" Narrow tailoring in this context requires, in other words, that the means chosen do not "burden substantially more speech than is necessary to further the government's legitimate interests."

Congress declared that the must-carry provisions serve three interrelated interests: (1) preserving the benefits of free, over-the-air local broadcast television, (2) promoting the widespread dissemination of information from a multiplicity of sources, and (3) promoting fair competition in the market for television programming. None of these interests is related to the "suppression of free expression," *O'Brien*, or to the content of any speakers' messages. And viewed in the abstract, we have no difficulty concluding that each of them is an important governmental interest.

That the Government's asserted interests are important in the abstract does not mean, however, that the must-carry rules will in fact advance those interests. When the Government defends a regulation on speech as a means to redress past harms or prevent anticipated harms, it must do more than simply "posit the existence of the disease sought to be cured." It must demonstrate that the recited harms are real, not merely conjectural, and that the regulation will in fact alleviate these harms in a direct and material way.

Thus, in applying *O'Brien* scrutiny we must ask first whether the Government has adequately shown that the economic health of local broadcasting is in genuine jeopardy and in need of the protections afforded by must-carry. Assuming an affirmative answer to the foregoing question, the Government still bears the burden of showing that the remedy it has adopted does not "burden substantially more speech than is necessary to further the government's legitimate interests." On the state of the record developed thus far, and in the absence of findings of fact from the District Court, we are unable to conclude that the Government has satisfied either inquiry.

In an opinion dissenting in part and joined by Justices Scalia, Ginsburg, and Thomas, however, Justice O'Connor contended that the "must-carry" provisions were content-based and thus "an impermissible restraint on the cable operators' editorial discretion as well as on the cable programmers' speech. For reasons related to the content of speech, the rules restrict the ability of cable operators to put on the programming they prefer, and require them to include programming they would rather avoid. . . . Assuming arguendo that the provisions are justified with reference to the content-neutral interests in fair competition and preservation of free television, they nonetheless restrict too much speech that does not implicate these interests."

H. SYMBOLIC SPEECH AND SPEECH-PLUS-CONDUCT

In a major ruling on freedom of speech and speech-plus-conduct growing out of the continuing controversy over abortion, the Rehnquist Court confronted the issue of anti-abortion protesters' First Amendment freedoms in *Madsen v. Women's Health Center*, 114 S.Ct. — (1994). *Madsen* presented the issue of whether a Florida trial judge's injunction against anti-abortion protesters constituted a suppression of their message or, as the Florida state supreme court held, aimed at protecting constitutionally guaranteed interests in medical care and patients' privacy. The trial judge forbid demonstrations within thirty-six feet of abortion clinics, prohibited protesters from coming into contact with women going into clinics within three hundred feet of the clinics, and banned all "congregating, picketing, patrolling, [and] demonstrating" within three hundred feet of the home of any doctors or other personnel who worked at an abortion clinic.

Splitting six to three and five to four on different parts of the ruling, the Court held that injunctions restraining protesters must be evaluated for the "content neutrality" and must not burden demonstrators' speech more than necessary to achieve the government's legitimate interests, as well as be framed in the narrowest terms to achieve its pin-point objective. Writing for the majority, Chief Justice Rehnquist upheld the thirty-six-foot buffer zone around the clinic's entrances and driveway, along with the limitations on noise around the clinic during surgery and recovery periods. However, he rejected as too broad and as an infringement on First Amendment freedoms the injunction's (1) thirty-six-foot buffer zone as applied to private property north and west of the clinic, (2) blanket ban on "observable images," and (3) three-hundred-foot no-approach zone around the clinic. Justice Souter filed a brief concurring opinion, and Justice Stevens filed an opinion in part concurring and dissenting. In a bitter dissent joined by Justices Kennedy and Thomas, Justice Scalia took strong exception to the majority's upholding any part of the injunction.

Madsen v. Women's Health Center

114 S.Ct. — (1994)

In 1993, after repeated demonstrations and arrests of anti-abortion protesters, the directors of the Aware Woman Center for Choice in Melbourne, Florida, sought an injuction stopping the protesters from going on their driveway and the surrounding street, as well as from harassing women and doctors entering the clinic. Judy Madsen and several other

Operation Rescue leaders named in the suit countered that such an injunction would deny them their First Amendment right of free speech. But, trial Judge Robert McGregor disagreed and issued an injunction creating a "buffer zone" around the clinic. The injunction forbid demonstrations within thirty-six feet of the clinic, prohibited anti-abortion protesters' contact with clinic clients and doctors, and banned "approaching, congregating, picketing, patrolling, [and] demonstrating" within three hundred feet of the home of any clinic personnel. In addition, Judge McGregor forbade in morning hours, "during surgical procedures and recovery periods," the protesters' singing, chanting, whistling, shouting, and use of bullhorns on the ground that such activities were too disruptive and threatened the women's psychological and physical well-being.

On appeal, the state supreme court upheld the injunction upon concluding that the anti-abortion protesters' tactics "placed in jeopardy the health, safety, and rights of Florida women" and "in light of the medical services provided at the clinic and Operation Rescue's past conduct." The First Amendment freedoms of the protesters were not denied, the state court reasoned, but instead merely subjected to reasonable "time, place, and manner" restrictions. By contrast, in a separate suit filed in the federal courts, the Court of Appeals for the Eleventh Circuit ruled that the injunction was an unconstitutional infringement on free speech in a "public forum." On Madsen's further appeal of the state court's ruling, the Supreme Court granted review in order to resolve the judicial conflict over the issue of the First Amendment rights of anti-abortion protesters.

Oral arguments before the Supreme Court prompted some of the most lively questioning from the bench during the term. Madsen's attorney, Mathew Staver, had a tough time arguing that the protesters were denied their freedom of speech, however. He also drew criticism for not sticking to the facts and falling back on First Amendment generalities. "Your argument is so confusing," observed Justice O'Connor at one point during his half-hour before the Court. Justice Souter rebuffed Staver's contention that the injunction denied his clients the right to speak outside of the clinic by asking him to read out loud the part of the injunction barring protesters from contacting clinic personnel and clients "unless such person indicates a desire to communicate." Souter, then, injected, "I don't see anything that prevents your clients from talking."

The clinic's lawyer, Talbot D'Alemberte, confronted no less sharp and skeptical questioning. Contrary to his claim that women entering the clinic were forced to run a "gantlet," Justice Kennedy noted that he found the demonstrations on a videotape to be "very orderly." When D'Alemberte pressed ahead arguing that the injunction aimed not at what the protesters said but at what they did, Justice Scalia cut him off. "You know what kind of speech your stopping," charged Scalia, "Any injunction against this group is *de facto* content-directed." Later, when Solicitor General Drew Days, who represented the Clinton administration as a "friend of the

Court" on the side of the clinic, asserted that Operation Rescue was simply out to intimidate the clinic's clients and staff, Scalia called his bluff. "Calling names is designed to hurt," said the justice, adding, "Calling President Nixon a murderer during the war in Vietnam was designed to hurt. But it wasn't unlawful." Justice Scalia also scoffed at D'Alemberte's claim that the "buffer zone" was necessary to secure a "tranquil environment" and to safeguard the clinic's clients' health. Could he protect himself, Scalia wondered aloud, by carrying a poster that read "Heart Condition: Do Not Upset Me?" Conceding that Justice Scalia could not, D'Alemberte and Days each tried to advance their position that the "buffer zone" was a legitimate "time, place, and manner" limitation, drawing mixed views from the bench. Justice Ginsburg reminded the Court that in the 1970s lower courts had refused to block a Nazi march in Skokie, Illinois, even though residents contended that the march would cause them to be "psychologically upset and physically sick." In contrast, Justice O'Connor observed that the Court had never before approved such injunctions as a "time, place, and manner" restriction and added, "Maybe we should."

The Court's decision was six to three and five to four on different parts of its ruling. Chief Justice Rehnquist delivered the majority's opinion. Justice Souter filed a concurring opinion and Justice Stevens issued an opinion in part concurring and dissenting. In a separate opinion in part concurring and dissenting, Justice Scalia was joined by Justices Kennedy and Thomas.

Chief Justice REHNQUIST delivered the opinion of the Court.

Petitioners challenge the constitutionality of an injunction entered by a Florida state court which prohibits antiabortion protestors from demonstrating in certain places and in various ways outside of a health clinic that performs abortions. We hold that the establishment of a 36-foot buffer zone on a public street from which demonstrators are excluded passes muster under the First Amendment, but that several other provisions of the injunction do not. . . .

II

We begin by addressing petitioners' contention that the state court's order, because it is an injunction that restricts only the speech of antiabortion protesters, is necessarily content or viewpoint based. Accordingly, they argue, we should examine the entire injunction under the strictest standard of scrutiny. We disagree. To accept petitioners' claim would be to classify virtually every injunction as content or viewpoint based. An injunction, by its very nature, applies only to a particular group (or individuals) and regulates the activities, and perhaps the speech, of that group. It does so, however, because of the group's past actions in the context of a specific dispute between real parties. The parties seeking the injunction assert a violation of their rights; the court hearing the action is charged with fashioning a remedy for a specific deprivation, not with the drafting of a statute addressed to the general public. . . .

Our principal inquiry in determining content neutrality is whether the government has adopted a regulation of speech "without reference to the content of the regulated speech." *Ward v. Rock Against Racism*, 491 U. S. 781 (1989). We thus look to the government's purpose as the threshold consideration. Here, the state court imposed restrictions on petitioners incidental to their antiabortion message because they repeatedly violated the court's original order. That petitioners all share the same viewpoint regarding abortion does not in itself demonstrate that some invidious content- or viewpoint-based purpose motivated the issuance of the order. It suggests only that those in the group whose conduct violated the court's order happen to share the same opinion regarding abortions being performed at the clinic. In short, the fact that the injunction covered people with a particular viewpoint does not itself render the injunction content or viewpoint based. Accordingly, the injunction issued in this case does not demand the level of heightened scrutiny . . . . And we proceed to discuss the standard which does govern.

III

If this were a content-neutral, generally applicable statute, instead of an injunctive order, its constitutionality would be assessed under the standard set forth in *Ward v. Rock Against Racism*, and similar cases. Given that the forum around the clinic is a traditional public forum, we would determine whether the time, place, and manner regulations were "narrowly tailored to serve a significant governmental interest." *Ward*. There are obvious differences, however, between an injunction and a generally applicable ordinance. Ordinances represent a legislative choice regarding the promotion of particular societal interests. Injunctions, by contrast, are remedies imposed for violations (or threatened violations) of a legislative or judicial decree. . . .

We believe that these differences require a somewhat more stringent application of general First Amendment principles in this context. . . . [W]hen evaluating a content-neutral injunction, we think that our standard time, place, and manner analysis is not sufficiently rigorous. We must ask instead whether the challenged provisions of the injunction burden no more speech than necessary to serve a significant government interest.

Both Justice STEVENS and Justice SCALIA disagree with the standard we announce, for policy reasons. Justice STEVENS believes that "injunctive relief should be judged by a more lenient standard than legislation," because injunctions are imposed on individuals or groups who have engaged in illegal activity. Justice SCALIA, by contrast, believes that content-neutral injunctions are "at least as deserving of strict scrutiny as a statutory, content-based restriction." Justice SCALIA bases his belief on the danger that injunctions, even though they might not "attack content as content," may be used to suppress particular ideas; that individual judges should not be trusted to impose injunctions in this context; and that an injunction is procedurally more difficult to challenge than a statute. We believe that consideration of all of the differences and similarities between statutes and injunctions supports, as a matter of policy, the standard we apply here. . . .

We begin with the 36-foot buffer zone. . . . The 36-foot buffer zone protecting the entrances to the clinic and the parking lot is a means of protecting unfettered ingress to and egress from the clinic, and ensuring that petitioners do not block traffic on Dixie Way. The state court seems to have had few other options to protect access given the narrow confines around the clinic. As the Florida Supreme Court noted, Dixie Way is only 21 feet wide in the area of the clinic. The state court was convinced that allowing the petitioners to remain on the clinic's sidewalk and driveway was not a viable option in view of the failure of the first injunction to protect access. And allowing the petitioners to stand in the middle of Dixie Way would obviously block vehicular traffic.

The need for a complete buffer zone near the clinic entrances and driveway may be debatable, but some deference must be given to the state court's familiarity with the facts and the background of the dispute between the parties even under our heightened review. Moreover, one of petitioners' witnesses during the evidentiary hearing before the state court conceded that the buffer zone was narrow enough to place petitioners at a distance of no greater than 10 to 12 feet from cars approaching and leaving the clinic. Protesters standing across the narrow street from the clinic can still be seen and heard from the clinic parking lots. We also bear in mind the fact that the state court originally issued a much narrower injunction, providing no buffer zone, and that this order did not succeed in protecting access to the clinic. The failure of the first order to accomplish its purpose may be taken into consideration in evaluating the constitutionality of the broader order. On balance, we hold that the 36-foot buffer zone around the clinic entrances and driveway burdens no more speech than necessary to accomplish the governmental interest at stake.

Justice SCALIA's dissent argues that a videotape made of demonstrations at the clinic represents "what one must presume to be the worst of the activity justifying the injunction." This seems to us a gratuitous assumption. The videotape was indeed introduced by respondents, presumably because they thought it supported their request for the second injunction. But witnesses also testified as to relevant facts in a 3-day evidentiary hearing, and the state court was therefore not limited to Justice SCALIA'S rendition of what he saw on the videotape to make its findings in support of the second injunction. Indeed, petitioners themselves studiously refrained from challenging the factual basis for the injunction both in the state courts and here. Before the Florida Supreme Court, petitioners stated that "the Amended Permanent Injunction contains fundamental error on its face. The sole question presented by this appeal is a question of law, and for purposes of this appeal [petitioners] are assuming, *arguendo*, that a factual basis exists to grant injunctive relief." Petitioners argued against including the factual record as an appendix in the Florida Supreme Court, and never certified a full record. We must therefore judge this case on the assumption that the evidence and testimony presented to the state court supported its findings that the presence of protesters standing, marching, and demonstrating near the clinic's entrance interfered with ingress to and egress from the clinic despite the issuance of the earlier injunction.

The inclusion of private property on the back and side of the clinic in the 36-foot buffer zone raises different concerns. . . . Patients and staff wishing to reach the clinic do not have to cross the private property abutting the clinic property on the north and west, and nothing in the record indicates that petitioners' activities on the private property have obstructed access to the clinic. Nor was evidence presented that protestors located on the private property blocked vehicular traffic on Dixie Way. Absent evidence that petitioners standing on the private property have obstructed access to the clinic, blocked vehicular traffic, or otherwise unlawfully interfered with the clinic's operation, this portion of the buffer zone fails to serve the significant government interests relied on by the Florida Supreme Court. We hold that on the record before us the 36-foot buffer zone as applied to the private property to the north and west of the clinic burdens more speech than necessary to protect access to the clinic.

In response to high noise levels outside the clinic, the state court restrained the petitioners from "singing, chanting, whistling, shouting, yelling, use of bullhorns, auto horns, sound amplification equipment or other sounds or images observable to or within earshot of the patients inside the clinic" during the hours of 7:30 a.m. through noon on Mondays through Saturdays. We must, of course, take account of the place to which the regulations apply in determining whether these restrictions burden more speech than necessary. We have upheld similar noise restrictions in the past, and as we noted in upholding a local noise ordinance around public schools, "the nature of a place, 'the pattern of its normal activities, dictate the kinds of regulations . . . that are reasonable.'" *Grayned v. City of Rockford*, 408 U. S. 104 (1972). . . . We hold that the limited noise restrictions imposed by the state court order burden no more speech than necessary to ensure the health and well-being of the patients at the clinic. The First Amendment does not demand that patients at a medical facility undertake Herculean efforts to escape the cacophony of political protests. "If overamplified loudspeakers assault the citizenry, government may turn them down." *Grayned*. That is what the state court did here, and we hold that its action was proper.

The same, however, cannot be said for the "images observable" provision of the state court's order. Clearly, threats to patients or their families, however communicated, are proscribable under the First Amendment. But rather than prohibiting the display of signs that could be interpreted as threats or veiled threats, the state court issued a blanket ban on all "images observable." This broad prohibition on all "images observable" burdens more speech than necessary to achieve the purpose of limiting threats to clinic patients or their families. Similarly, if the blanket ban on "images observable" was intended to reduce the level of anxiety and hypertension suffered by the patients inside the clinic, it would still fail. The only plausible reason a patient would be bothered by "images observable" inside the clinic would be if the patient found the expression contained in such images disagreeable. But it is much easier for the clinic to pull its curtains than for a patient to stop up her ears, and no more is required to avoid seeing placards through the windows of the clinic. This provision of the injunction violates the First Amendment.

The state court ordered that petitioners refrain from physically approaching any person seeking services of the clinic "unless such person indicates a desire to communicate" in an area within 300 feet of the clinic. But it is difficult, indeed, to justify a prohibition on all uninvited approaches of persons seeking the services of the clinic, regardless of how peaceful the contact may be, without burdening more speech than necessary to prevent intimidation and to ensure access to the clinic. Absent evidence that the protesters' speech is independently proscribable (i.e., "fighting words" or threats), or is so infused with violence as to be indistinguishable from a threat of physical harm, this provision cannot stand.

The final substantive regulation challenged by petitioners relates to a prohibition against picketing, demonstrating, or using sound amplification equipment within 300 feet of the residences of clinic staff. The prohibition also covers impeding access to streets that provide the sole access to streets on which those residences are located. The same analysis applies to the use of sound amplification equipment here as that discussed above: the government may simply demand that petitioners turn down the volume if the protests overwhelm the neighborhood.

As for the picketing, our prior decision upholding a law banning targeted residential picketing remarked on the unique nature of the home, as "'the last citadel of the tired, the weary, and the sick.'" [*Frisby v. Schultz*, 487 U.S. 474 (1988)]. We stated that "'the State's interest in protecting the well-being, tranquility, and privacy of the home is certainly of the highest order in a free and civilized society.'"

By contrast, the 300-foot zone would ban "general marching through residential neighborhoods, or even walking a route in front of an entire block of houses." The record before us does not contain sufficient justification for this broad a ban on picketing; it appears that a limitation on the time, duration of picketing, and number of pickets outside a smaller zone could have accomplished the desired result. . . .

V

In sum, we uphold the noise restrictions and the 36-foot buffer zone around the clinic entrances and driveway because they burden no more speech than necessary to eliminate the unlawful conduct targeted by the state court's injunction. We strike down as unconstitutional the 36-foot buffer zone as applied to the private property to the north and west of the clinic, the "images observable" provision, the 300-foot no-approach zone around the clinic, and the 300-foot buffer zone around the residences, because these provisions sweep more broadly than necessary to accomplish the permissible goals of the injunction. Accordingly, the judgment of the Florida Supreme Court is

Affirmed in part, and reversed in part.

Justice STEVENS, concurring in part and dissenting in part.

The *certiorari* petition presented three questions, corresponding to petitioners' three major challenges to the trial court's injunction. The Court correctly and unequivocally rejects petitioners' argument that the injunction is a "content-based restriction on free speech," as well as their challenge to the injunction on the basis that it applies to persons acting "in concert" with them. I therefore join Parts II and IV of the Court's opinion, which properly dispose of the first and third questions presented. I part company with the Court, however, on its treatment of the second question presented, including its enunciation of the applicable standard of review.

I agree with the Court that a different standard governs First Amendment challenges to generally applicable legislation than the standard that measures such challenges to judicial remedies for proven wrongdoing. Unlike the Court, however, I believe that injunctive relief should be judged by a more lenient standard than legislation. As the Court notes, legislation is imposed on an entire community, regardless of individual culpability. By contrast, injunctions apply solely to an individual or a limited group of individuals who, by engaging in illegal conduct, have been judicially deprived of some liberty–the normal consequence of illegal activity. Given this distinction, a statute prohibiting demonstrations within 36 feet of an abortion clinic would probably violate the First Amendment, but an injunction directed at a limited group of persons who have engaged in unlawful conduct in a similar zone might well be constitutional. . . .

Justice SCALIA, with whom Justice KENNEDY and Justice THOMAS join, concurring in the judgment in part and dissenting in part.

The judgment in today's case has an appearance of moderation and Solomonic wisdom, upholding as it does some portions of the injunction while disallowing others. That appearance is deceptive. The entire injunction in this case departs so far from the established course of our jurisprudence that in any other context it would have been regarded as a candidate for summary reversal. But the context here is abortion. . . .

Because I believe that the judicial creation of a 36-foot zone in which only a particular group, which had broken no law, cannot exercise its rights of speech, assembly, and association, and the judicial enactment of a noise prohibition, applicable to that group and that group alone, are profoundly at odds with our First Amendment precedents and traditions, I dissent.

The record of this case contains a videotape, with running caption of time and date, displaying what one must presume to be the worst of the activity justifying the injunction issued by Judge McGregor and partially approved today by this Court. The tape was shot by employees of, or volunteers at, the Aware Woman Clinic on three Saturdays in February and March 1993; the camera location, for the first and third segments, appears to have been an upper floor of the clinic. The tape was edited down (from approximately 6 to 8 hours of footage to 1/2 hour) by Ruth Arick, a management consultant employed by the clinic and by the Feminist Majority Foundation. Anyone seriously interested in what this case was about must view that tape. And anyone doing so who is familiar with run-of-the-mine labor picketing, not to mention some other social protests, will be aghast at what it shows we have today permitted an individual judge to do. . . .

The videotape and the rest of the record, including the trial court's findings, show that a great many forms of expression and conduct occurred in the vicinity of the clinic. These include singing, chanting, praying, shouting, the playing of music both from the clinic and from handheld boom boxes, speeches, peaceful picketing, communication of familiar political messages, handbilling, persuasive speech directed at opposing groups on the issue of abortion, efforts to persuade individuals not to have abortions, personal testimony, interviews with the press, and media efforts to report on the protest. What the videotape, the rest of the record, and the trial court's findings do not contain is any suggestion of violence near the clinic, nor do they establish any attempt to prevent entry or exit.

Under this Court's jurisprudence, there is no question that this public sidewalk area is a "public forum," where citizens generally have a First Amendment right to speak. The parties to this case invited the Court to employ one or the other of the two well established standards applied to restrictions upon this First Amendment right. Petitioners claimed the benefit of so-called "strict scrutiny," the standard applied to content-based restrictions: the restriction must be "necessary to serve a compelling state interest and . . . narrowly drawn to achieve that end." *Perry Education Assn. v. Perry Local Educators' Assn.*, 460 U. S. 37 (1983). Respondents, on the other hand, contended for what has come to be known as "intermediate scrutiny" (midway between the "strict scrutiny" demanded for content-based regulation of speech, and the "rational basis" standard that is applied–under the Equal Protection Clause–to government regulation of non-speech activities). That standard, applicable to so-called "time, place and manner regulations" of speech, provides that the regulations are permissible so long as they "are content-neutral, are narrowly tailored to serve a significant government interest, and leave open ample alternative channels of communication." The Court adopts neither of these, but creates, brand-new for this abortion-related case, an additional standard that is (supposedly) "somewhat more stringent," than intermediate scrutiny, yet not as "rigorous," as strict scrutiny. The Court does not give this new standard a name, but perhaps we could call it intermediate-intermediate scrutiny. The difference between it and intermediate scrutiny (which the Court acknowledges is inappropriate for injunctive restrictions on speech) is frankly too subtle for me to describe, so I must simply recite it: whereas intermediate scrutiny requires that the restriction be "narrowly tailored to serve a significant government interest," the new standard requires that the restriction "burden no more speech than necessary to serve a significant government interest." . . .

The danger of content-based statutory restrictions upon speech is that they may be designed and used precisely to suppress the ideas in question rather than to achieve any other proper governmental aim. But that same danger exists with injunctions. Although a speech-restricting injunction may not attack content as content (in the present case, as I shall discuss, even that is not true), it lends itself just as readily to the targeted suppression of particular ideas. When a judge, on the motion of an employer, enjoins picketing at the site of a labor dispute, he enjoins (and he knows he is enjoining) the expression of pro-union views. Such targeting of one or the other side of an ideological dispute cannot readily be achieved in speech-restricting general legislation except by making content the basis of the restriction; it is achieved in speech-restricting injunctions almost invariably. The proceedings before us here illustrate well enough what I mean. The injunction was sought against a single-issue advocacy group by persons and organizations with a business or social interest in suppressing that group's point of view.

The second reason speech-restricting injunctions are at least as deserving of strict scrutiny is obvious enough: they are the product of individual judges rather than of legislatures—and often of judges who have been chagrined by prior disobedience of their orders. The right to free speech should not lightly be placed within the control of a single man or woman. And the third reason is that the injunction is a much more powerful weapon than a statute, and so should be subjected to greater safeguards. . . .

The proposition that injunctions against speech are subject to a standard indistinguishable from (unless perhaps more lenient in its application than) the "intermediate scrutiny" standard we have used for "time, place, and manner" legislative restrictions; the notion that injunctions against speech need not be closely tied to any violation of law, but may simply implement sound social policy; and the practice of accepting trial-court conclusions permitting injunctions without considering whether those conclusions are supported by any findings of fact—these latest by-products of our abortion jurisprudence ought to give all friends of liberty great concern.

For these reasons, I dissent from that portion of the judgment upholding parts of the injunction.

6

FREEDOM FROM AND OF RELIGION

A. THE (DIS)ESTABLISHMENT OF RELIGION

In a number of cases in recent years the Rehnquist Court has reconsidered the First Amendment's guarantees for religious freedom (see Vol. 2, Ch. 6). Moreover, a number of the justices have frequently expressed dissatisfaction with the three-pronged test for applying the (dis)establishment clause set forth by the Burger Court in *Lemon v. Kurtzman*, 403 U.S. 604 (1971) (in Vol. 2, Ch. 6). Under *Lemon*, governmental legislation and regulations must (1) have a secular purpose, (2) have a primary effect that neither advances nor inhibits religion, and (3) not foster an excessive governmental entanglement with religion. But, Chief Justice Rehnquist and Justice Scalia, in particular, have pushed for a greater accommodation of religion by the government and for overruling *Lemon*. Still, even with its changing composition, the Court has been unable to agree on whether to jettison or to adhere to *Lemon*, as well as on how and when to apply the test. As a result, the Court's rulings on the (dis)establishment clause have been fragmented, confusing, and have invited continued litigation.

In spite of calls from within and without the Court to overturn *Lemon*, in *Lee v. Weisman*, 112 S.Ct. 2649 (1992) (in Vol. 2, Ch. 6), a bare majority declined to do so, when holding that school-sponsored prayers at graduation ceremonies run afoul of the (dis)establishment clause. Last term, then, in two more cases the Court declined to reexamine *Lemon*. In *Lamb's Chapel v. Center Moriches Union Free School District*, 113 S.Ct. 2141 (1993) (in Vol. 2, Ch. 6), the Court unanimously held that the denial by a school district of a religious group's use of public school facilities for meetings after school hours violated the First Amendment. And in *Zobrest v. Catalina Foothills School District*, 113 S.Ct. 2462 (1993) (in Vol. 2, Ch. 6), a bare majority ruled that there is no bar against public funding for a sign-language interpeter for a deaf student who attends a religious school.

Once again, in its 1993-1994 term, the Court was asked to jettison *Lemon* in *Board of Education of Kiryas Joel v. Grumet*, 114 S.Ct. — (1994) (excerpted below). Notably, though, the Court declined again to abandon

Lemon. Dividing six to three when striking down New York's law creating a special school district for Kiryas Joel, Justice Souter's opinion for the Court twice noted approvingly the ruling in *Lemon*. His opinion in parts, however, commanded only a plurality of the justices. Justice Blackmun issued a brief concurring opinion strongly supporting the *Lemon* test, while Justice O'Connor's concurring opinion, again, suggested that *Lemon* should be abandoned. Joined by Chief Justice Rehnquist and Justice Thomas, dissenting Justice Scalia also renewed his call for abandoning *Lemon*.

Board of Education of Kiryas Joel Village School District v. Grumet

114 S.Ct. — (1994)

In response to a ruling by a bare majority of the Supreme Court in *Aguilar v. Felton*, 473 U.S. 402 (1985), forbidding public school teachers from offering remedial classes for handicapped children attending religious schools, the New York legislature created a special school district, governed by the Board of Education of Kiryas Joel, in Orange County, New York. Kiryas Joel is a community solely of Hasidic Jews of the Satmar sect, one of the most orthodox and conservative Jewish sects. All other Jewish children in the district attended private religious schools. But Kiryas Joel did not want to send two hundred handicapped children to public schools in the county because that might expose them to stress and possible ridicule for their clothes, use of Yiddish, and other traditional practices. In 1989, the state legislature created a special public school district for Kiryas Joel's handicapped children. The following year, Louis Grumet, the director of the New York State School Boards, challenged the constitutionality of the special school district as a violation of the First Amendment's (dis)establishment clause. Lower state courts and the New York Court of Appeals agreed that the special district failed to pass the tests set forth in *Lemon v. Kurtzman*, 403 U.S. 602 (1971) (in Vol. 2, Ch. 6), specifically, those requiring that legislation have a primary effect that neither advances nor inhibits religion. The school district thereupon appealed to the Supreme Court.

During oral arguments before the high court, the school board's attorney, Nathan Lewin, argued, on the one hand, that the district was "wholly secular" in serving only the special educational needs of disabled children, and therefore did not violate the (dis)establishment clause. Lewin, on the other hand, also insisted that the First Amendment's free exercise clause guaranteed Kiryas Joel the right to operate the schools. "It turns the Constitution on its head," as he put it, "to say that the free exercise of religion becomes the one impermissible vice" that triggers the (dis)establishment clause and renders the district unconstitutional.

Those arguments drew mixed reactions from the bench. Justice O'Connor, for one, was troubled by the fact that the district was not set up under generally applicable legislation. Instead, the school district had been created in response to the demands of the Satmar sect, and she suggested that that presented a "dangerous precedent." By contrast, Justice Scalia charged that religion wasn't even an issue in the case. As he pointed out to Grumet's attorney, "Their customs spring out of their religion, but the state was accommodating their customs. I don't see how the state is accommodating any religious beliefs." Yet, Grumet's counsel maintained that the Satmar's culture "can't be distinguished from their religious precepts" and characterized the school district as "a political constituency defined by religious lines." That in turn prompted disagreement from Chief Justice Rehnquist, who shot back: "You're saying that the Satmars, because they all live together, can't exercise the same governmental authority that other people living together would be able to exercise." Why could not a group of Roman Catholics get together and say, Rehnquist asked, "We think pretty much alike and we'd like our own school district?" Perhaps that would be constitutional, responded Grumet's attorney, but here the state created the Kiryas Joel district in order "to let a religious community dictate where educational services would take place."

The Court's decision was six to three. Justice Souter announced the majority's opinion, which Justices Blackmun, Stevens, O'Connor, and Ginsburg joined in Parts I, II-B, II-C, and III, and which Justices Blackmun, Stevens, and Ginsburg joined in Parts II-A. Justices Blackmun, Stevens, Kennedy, and O'Connor filed separate concurring opinions. Justice Scalia filed a dissenting opinion, which Chief Justice Rehnquist and Justice Thomas joined.

Justice SOUTER delivered the opinion of the Court.

The question is whether the Act creating the separate school district violates the Establishment Clause of the First Amendment, binding on the States through the Fourteenth Amendment. Because this unusual act is tantamount to an allocation of political power on a religious criterion and neither presupposes nor requires governmental impartiality toward religion, we hold that it violates the prohibition against establishment. . . .

II

"A proper respect for both the Free Exercise and the Establishment Clauses compels the State to pursue a course of 'neutrality' toward religion," *Committee for Public Ed. & Religious Liberty v. Nyquist*, 413 U. S. 756 (1973), favoring neither one religion over others nor religious adherents collectively over nonadherents. Chapter 748, the statute creating the Kiryas Joel Village School District, departs from this constitutional command by delegating the State's discretionary authority over public schools to a group defined by its character as a religious community, in a legal and historical context that gives no assurance that governmental power has been or will be exercised neutrally.

Larkin v. Grendel's Den, Inc., 459 U. S. 116 (1982), provides an instructive comparison with the litigation before us. There, the Court was requested to strike down a Massachusetts statute granting religious bodies veto power over applications for liquor licenses. Under the statute, the governing body of any church, synagogue, or school located within 500 feet of an applicant's premises could, simply by submitting written objection, prevent the Alcohol Beverage Control Commission from issuing a license. In spite of the State's valid interest in protecting churches, schools, and like institutions from "'the hurly-burly' associated with liquor outlets," the Court found that in two respects the statute violated "the wholesome 'neutrality' of which this Court's cases speak," *School Dist. of Abington v. Schempp*, 374 U. S. 203 (1963). The Act brought about a "'fusion of governmental and religious functions'" by delegating "important, discretionary governmental powers" to religious bodies, thus impermissibly entangling government and religion. And it lacked "any 'effective means of guaranteeing' that the delegated power '[would] be used exclusively for secular, neutral, and nonideological purposes;'" this, along with the "significant symbolic benefit to religion" associated with "the mere appearance of a joint exercise of legislative authority by Church and State," led the Court to conclude that the statute had a "'primary' and 'principal' effect of advancing religion." Comparable constitutional problems inhere in the statute before us.

A

Larkin presented an example of united civic and religious authority, an establishment rarely found in such straightforward form in modern America. The Establishment Clause problem presented by Chapter 748 is more subtle, but it resembles the issue raised in *Larkin* to the extent that the earlier case teaches that a State may not delegate its civic authority to a group chosen according to a religious criterion. Authority over public schools belongs to the State, and cannot be delegated to a local school district defined by the State in order to grant political control to a religious group. What makes this litigation different from *Larkin* is the delegation here of civic power to the "qualified voters of the village of Kiryas Joel," as distinct from a religious leader such as the village rov, or an institution of religious government like the formally constituted parish council in *Larkin*. In light of the circumstances of this case, however, this distinction turns out to lack constitutional significance.

It is, first, not dispositive that the recipients of state power in this case are a group of religious individuals united by common doctrine, not the group's leaders or officers. Although some school district franchise is common to all voters, the State's manipulation of the franchise for this district limited it to

Satmars, giving the sect exclusive control of the political subdivision. In the circumstances of this case, the difference between thus vesting state power in the members of a religious group as such instead of the officers of its sectarian organization is one of form, not substance. It is true that religious people (or groups of religious people) cannot be denied the opportunity to exercise the rights of citizens simply because of their religious affiliations or commitments, for such a disability would violate the right to religious free exercise, see *McDaniel v. Paty*, 435 U. S. 618 (1978), which the First Amendment guarantees as certainly as it bars any establishment. But *McDaniel*, which held that a religious individual could not, because of his religious activities, be denied the right to hold political office, is not in point here. That individuals who happen to be religious may hold public office does not mean that a state may deliberately delegate discretionary power to an individual, institution, or community on the ground of religious identity. If New York were to delegate civic authority to "the Grand Rebbe," *Larkin* would obviously require invalidation (even though under *McDaniel* the Grand Rebbe may run for, and serve on his local school board), and the same is true if New York delegates political authority by reference to religious belief. Where "fusion" is an issue, the difference lies in the distinction between a government's purposeful delegation on the basis of religion and a delegation on principles neutral to religion, to individuals whose religious identities are incidental to their receipt of civic authority.

Of course, Chapter 748 delegates power not by express reference to the religious belief of the Satmar community, but to residents of the "territory of the village of Kiryas Joel." Thus the second (and arguably more important) distinction between this case and *Larkin* is the identification here of the group to exercise civil authority in terms not expressly religious. But our analysis does not end with the text of the statute at issue, see *Church of Lukumi Babalu Aye, Inc. v. Hialeah*, 508 U. S. – (1993); *Wallace v. Jaffree*, 472 U. S. 38 (1985); *Gomillion v. Lightfoot*, 364 U. S. 339 (1960), and the context here persuades us that Chapter 748 effectively identifies these recipients of governmental authority by reference to doctrinal adherence, even though it does not do so expressly. We find this to be the better view of the facts because of the way the boundary lines of the school district divide residents according to religious affiliation, under the terms of an unusual and special legislative act.

It is undisputed that those who negotiated the village boundaries when applying the general village incorporation statute drew them so as to exclude all but Satmars, and that the New York Legislature was well aware that the village remained exclusively Satmar in 1989 when it adopted Chapter 748. The significance of this fact to the state legislature is indicated by the further fact that carving out the village school district ran counter to customary districting practices in the State. Indeed, the trend in New York is not toward dividing school districts but toward consolidating them. . . .

The origin of the district in a special act of the legislature, rather than the State's general laws governing school district reorganization, is likewise anomalous. . . . Because the district's creation ran uniquely counter to state practice, following the lines of a religious community where the customary and neutral principles would not have dictated the same result, we have good reasons to treat this district as the reflection of a religious criterion for identifying the recipients of civil authority. Not even the special needs of the children in this community can explain the legislature's unusual Act, for the State could have responded to the concerns of the Satmar parents without implicating the Establishment Clause, as we explain in some detail further on. We therefore find the legislature's Act to be substantially equivalent to defining a political subdivision and hence the qualification for its franchise by a religious test, resulting in a purposeful and forbidden "fusion of governmental and religious functions." *Larkin v. Grendel's Den.*

B

The fact that this school district was created by a special and unusual Act of the legislature also gives reason for concern whether the benefit received by the Satmar community is one that the legislature will provide equally to other religious (and nonreligious) groups. This is the second malady the *Larkin* Court identified in the law before it, the absence of an "effective means of guaranteeing" that governmental power will be and has been neutrally employed. But whereas in *Larkin* it was religious groups the Court thought might exercise civic power to advance the interests of religion (or religious adherents), here the threat to neutrality occurs at an antecedent stage.

The fundamental source of constitutional concern here is that the legislature itself may fail to exercise governmental authority in a religiously neutral way. The anomalously case-specific nature of the legislature's exercise of state authority in creating this district for a religious community leaves the Court without any direct way to review such state action for the purpose of safeguarding a principle at the heart of the Establishment Clause, that government should not prefer one religion to another, or religion to irreligion. Because the religious community of Kiryas Joel did not receive its new governmental authority simply as one of many communities eligible for equal treatment under a general law, we have no assurance that the next similarly situated group seeking a school district of its own will receive one; unlike an administrative agency's denial of an exemption from a generally applicable law, which "would be entitled to a judicial audience," a legislature's failure to enact a special law is itself unreviewable. Nor can the historical context in this case furnish us with any reason to suppose that the Satmars are merely one in a series of communities receiving the benefit of special school district laws. Early on in the development of public education in New York, the State rejected highly localized school districts for New York City when they were promoted as a way to allow separate schooling for Roman Catholic children. And in more recent history, the special Act in this case stands alone. The general principle that civil power must be exercised in a manner neutral to religion is one the *Larkin* Court recognized, although it did not discuss the specific possibility of legislative favoritism along religious lines because the statute before it delegated state authority to any religious group assembled near the premises of an applicant for a liquor license, as well as to a further category of institutions not identified by religion. But the principle is well grounded in our case law, as we have frequently relied explicitly on the general availability of any benefit provided religious groups or individuals in turning aside Establishment Clause challenges. . . . Here the benefit flows only to a single sect, but aiding this single, small religious group causes no less a constitutional problem than would follow from aiding a sect with more members or religion as a whole, and we are forced to conclude that the State of New York has violated the Establishment Clause.

C

In finding that Chapter 748 violates the requirement of governmental neutrality by extending the benefit of a special franchise, we do not deny that the Constitution allows the state to accommodate religious needs by alleviating special burdens. Our cases leave no doubt that in commanding neutrality the Religion Clauses do not require the government to be oblivious to impositions that legitimate exercises of state power may place on religious belief and practice. Rather, there is "ample room under the Establishment Clause for 'benevolent neutrality which will permit religious exercise to exist without sponsorship and without interference,'" *Corporation of Presiding Bishop of Church of Jesus Christ of Latter-day Saints v. Amos*, 483 U. S. 327 (1987). The fact that Chapter 748 facilitates the practice of religion is not what renders it an unconstitutional establishment.

But accommodation is not a principle without limits, and what petitioners seek is an adjustment to the Satmars' religiously grounded preferences that our cases do not countenance. Prior decisions have allowed religious communities and institutions to pursue their own interests free from governmental interference, but we have never hinted that an otherwise unconstitutional delegation of political power to a religious group could be saved as a religious accommodation. Petitioners' proposed accommodation singles out a particular religious sect for special treatment, and whatever the limits of permissible legislative accommodations may be, compare *Texas Monthly, Inc. v. Bullock*, (striking down law exempting only religious publications from taxation), with *Corporation of Presiding Bishop v. Amos*, (upholding law exempting religious employers from Title VII), it is clear that neutrality as among religions must be honored.

This conclusion does not, however, bring the Satmar parents, the Monroe-Woodbury school district, or the State of New York to the end of the road in seeking ways to respond to the parents' concerns. Just as the Court in *Larkin* observed that the State's interest in protecting religious meeting places could be "readily accomplished by other means," there are several alternatives here for providing bilingual and bicultural special education to Satmar children. Such services can perfectly well be offered to village children through the Monroe-Woodbury Central School District. Since the Satmars do not claim that separatism is religiously mandated, their children may receive bilingual and bicultural instruction at a public school already run by the Monroe-Woodbury district. Or if the educationally appropriate offering by Monroe-Woodbury should turn out to be a separate program of bilingual and bicultural education at a neutral site near one of the village's parochial schools, this Court has already made it clear that no Establishment Clause difficulty would inhere in such a scheme, administered in accordance with neutral principles that would not necessarily confine special treatment to Satmars. . . .

III

Justice CARDOZO once cast the dissenter as "the gladiator making a last stand against the lions." B. CARDOZO, *Law and Literature* 34 (1931). Justice SCALIA's dissent is certainly the work of a gladiator, but he thrusts at lions of his own imagining. We do not disable a religiously homogeneous group from exercising political power conferred on it without regard to religion. Unlike the states of Utah and New Mexico (which were laid out according to traditional political methodologies taking account of lines of latitude and longitude and topographical features), the reference line chosen for the Kiryas Joel Village School District was one purposely drawn to separate Satmars from non-Satmars. Nor do we impugn the motives of the New York Legislature, which no doubt intended to accommodate the Satmar community without vio-lating the Establishment Clause; we simply refuse to ignore that the method it chose is one that aids a particular religious community, as such, rather than all groups similarly interested in separate schooling. . . .

Our job, of course would be easier if the dissent's position had prevailed with the Framers and with this Court over the years. An Establishment Clause diminished to the dimensions acceptable to Justice SCALIA could be enforced by a few simple rules, and our docket would never see cases requiring the application of a principle like neutrality toward religion as well as among religious sects. But that would be as blind to history as to precedent, and the difference between Justice SCALIA and the Court accordingly turns on the Court's recognition that the Establishment Clause does comprehend such a principle and obligates courts to exercise the judgment necessary to apply it.

In this case we are clearly constrained to conclude that the statute before us fails the test of neutrality. It delegates a power this Court has said "ranks at the very apex of the function of a State," *Wisconsin v. Yoder*, 406 U. S. 205 (1972), to an electorate defined by common religious belief and practice, in a manner that fails to foreclose religious favoritism. It therefore crosses the line from permissible accommodation to impermissible establishment. The judgment of the Court of Appeals of the State of New York is accordingly

Affirmed.

Justice BLACKMUN, concurring.

I write separately only to note my disagreement with any suggestion that today's decision signals a departure from the principles described in *Lemon v. Kurtzman*, 403 U. S. 602 (1971). The opinion of the Court (and of the plurality with respect to Part II-A) relies upon several decisions, including

Larkin v. Grendel's Den, Inc., 459 U. S. 116 (1982), that explicitly rested on the criteria set forth in *Lemon*. Indeed, the two principles on which the opinion bases its conclusion that the legislative act is constitutionally invalid essentially are the second and third *Lemon* criteria. . . .

Justice O'CONNOR, concurring in part and concurring in the judgment.

We have time and again held that the government generally may not treat people differently based on the God or gods they worship, or don't worship. This emphasis on equal treatment is, I think, an eminently sound approach. In my view, the Religion Clauses—the Free Exercise Clause, the Establishment Clause, the Religious Test Clause, Art. VI, cl. 3, and the Equal Protection Clause as applied to religion—all speak with one voice on this point: Absent the most unusual circumstances, one's religion ought not affect one's legal rights or duties or benefits. As I have previously noted, "the Establishment Clause is infringed when the government makes adherence to religion relevant to a person's standing in the political community." *Wallace v. Jaffree*, 472 U. S. 38 (1985) (O'CONNOR, J., concurring in judgment).

That the government is acting to accommodate religion should generally not change this analysis. What makes accommodation permissible, even praiseworthy, is not that the government is making life easier for some particular religious group as such. Rather, it is that the government is accommodating a deeply held belief. Accommodations may thus justify treating those who share this belief differently from those who do not; but they do not justify discriminations based on sect. A state law prohibiting the consumption of alcohol may exempt sacramental wines, but it may not exempt sacramental wine use by Catholics but not by Jews. A draft law may exempt conscientious objectors, but it may not exempt conscientious objectors whose objections are based on theistic belief (such as Quakers) as opposed to nontheistic belief (such as Buddhists) or atheistic belief.

Experience proves that the Establishment Clause, like the Free Speech Clause, cannot easily be reduced to a single test. There are different categories of Establishment Clause cases, which may call for different approaches. Some cases, like this one, involve government actions targeted at particular individuals or groups, imposing special duties or giving special benefits. Cases involving government speech on religious topics, seem to me to fall into a different category and to require an analysis focusing on whether the speech endorses or disapproves of religion, rather than on whether the government action is neutral with regard to religion. Another category encompasses cases in which the government must make decisions about matters of religious doctrine and religious law. These cases, which often arise in the application of otherwise neutral property or contract principles to religious institutions, involve complicated questions not present in other situations. Government delegations of power to religious bodies may make up yet another category. As *Larkin* itself suggested, government impartiality towards religion may not be enough in such situations: A law that bars all alcohol sales within some distance of a church, school, or hospital may be valid, but an equally evenhanded law that gives each institution discretionary power over the sales may not be. Of course, there may well be additional categories, or more opportune places to draw the lines between the categories.

As the Court's opinion today shows, the slide away from *Lemon*'s unitary approach is well under way. A return to *Lemon*, even if possible, would likely be futile, regardless of where one stands on the substantive Establishment Clause questions. I think a less unitary approach provides a better structure for analysis. If each test covers a narrower and more homogeneous area, the tests may be more precise and therefore easier to apply. There may be more opportunity to pay attention to the specific nuances of each area. There might also be, I hope, more consensus on each of the narrow tests than there has been on a broad test. And abandoning the *Lemon* framework need not mean abandoning some of the insights that the test reflected, nor the insights of the cases that applied it. . . .

Justice KENNEDY, concurring in the judgment.

The Court's ruling that the Kiryas Joel Village School District violates the Establishment Clause is in my view correct, but my reservations about what the Court's reasoning implies for religious accommodations in general are sufficient to require a separate writing. As the Court recognizes, a legislative accommodation that discriminates among religions may become an establishment of religion. But the Court's opinion can be interpreted to say that an accommodation for a particular religious group is invalid because of the risk that the legislature will not grant the same accommodation to another religious group suffering some similar burden. This rationale seems to me without grounding in our precedents and a needless restriction upon the legislature's ability to respond to the unique problems of a particular religious group. The real vice of the school district, in my estimation, is that New York created it by drawing political boundaries on the basis of religion. I would decide the issue we confront upon this narrower theory, though in accord with many of the Court's general observations about the State's actions in this case. . . .

Justice SCALIA, with whom the CHIEF JUSTICE and Justice THOMAS join, dissenting.

The Court today finds that the Powers That Be, up in Albany, have conspired to effect an establishment of the Satmar Hasidim. I do not know who would be more surprised at this discovery: the Founders of our Nation or Grand Rebbe Joel Teitelbaum, founder of the Satmar. The Grand Rebbe would be astounded to learn that after escaping brutal persecution and coming to America with the modest hope of religious toleration for their ascetic form of Judaism, the Satmar had become so powerful, so closely allied with Mammon, as to have become an "establishment" of the Empire State. And the Founding Fathers would be astonished to find that the Establishment Clause—which they designed "to insure that no one powerful sect or combination of sects could use political or governmental power to punish dissenters," *Zorach v. Clauson*, 343 U. S. 306 (1952) (BLACK, J., dissenting)—has been employed to prohibit characteristically and admirably American accommodation of the religious practices (or more precisely, cultural peculiarities) of a tiny minority sect. I, however, am not surprised. Once this Court has abandoned text and history as guides, nothing prevents it from calling religious toleration the establishment of religion. . . .

For his thesis that New York has unconstitutionally conferred governmental authority upon the Satmar sect, Justice SOUTER relies extensively, and virtually exclusively, upon *Larkin v. Grendel's Den, Inc.*, 459 U. S. 116 (1982). Justice SOUTER believes that the present case "resembles" *Grendel's Den* because that cases "teaches that a state may not delegate its civic authority to a group chosen according to a religious criterion." That misdescribes both what that case taught (which is that a state may not delegate its civil authority to a church), and what this case involves (which is a group chosen according to cultural characteristics). The statute at issue there gave churches veto power over the State's authority to grant a liquor license to establishments in the vicinity of the church. The Court had little difficulty finding the statute unconstitutional.

Justice SOUTER concedes that *Grendel's Den* "presented an example of united civic and religious authority, an establishment rarely found in such straightforward form in modern America." The uniqueness of the case stemmed from the grant of governmental power directly to a religious institution, and the Court's opinion focused on that fact, remarking that the transfer of authority was to "churches" (10 times), the "governing body of churches" (twice), "religious institutions" (twice) and "religious bodies" (once). Astonishingly, however, Justice SOUTER dismisses the difference between a transfer of government power to citizens who share a common religion as opposed to "the officers of its sectarian organization"—the critical factor that made *Grendel's Den* unique and "rare"—as being "one of form, not substance."

Justice SOUTER's steamrolling of the difference between civil authority held by a church, and civil authority held by members of a church, is breathtaking. To accept it, one must believe that large portions of the civil authority exercised during most of our history were unconstitutional, and that much more of it than merely the Kiryas Joel School District is unconstitutional today. The history of the populating of North America is in no small measure the story of groups of people sharing a common religious and cultural heritage striking out to form their own communities. It is preposterous to suggest that the civil institutions of these communities, separate from their churches, were constitutionally suspect. And if they were, surely Justice SOUTER cannot mean that the inclusion of one or two nonbelievers in the community would have been enough to eliminate the constitutional vice. If the conferral of governmental power upon a religious institution as such (rather than upon American citizens who belong to the religious institution) is not the test of Grendel's Den invalidity, there is no reason why giving power to a body that is overwhelmingly dominated by the members of one sect would not suffice to invoke the Establishment Clause. That might have made the entire States of Utah and New Mexico unconstitutional at the time of their admission to the Union, and would undoubtedly make many units of local government unconstitutional today. [A census taken in 1906, 10 years after statehood was granted to Utah, and 6 years before it was granted to New Mexico, showed that in Utah 87.7% of all church members were Mormon, and in New Mexico 88.7% of all church members were Roman Catholic.]

Justice SOUTER's position boils down to the quite novel proposition that any group of citizens (say, the residents of Kiryas Joel) can be invested with political power, but not if they all belong to the same religion. Of course such disfavoring of religion is positively antagonistic to the purposes of the Religion Clauses, and we have rejected it before. In *McDaniel v. Paty*, 435 U. S. 618 (1978), we invalidated a state constitutional amendment that would have permitted all persons to participate in political conventions, except ministers. We adopted James Madison's view that the State could not " 'punish a religious profession with the privation of a civil right.' " I see no reason why it is any less pernicious to deprive a group rather than an individual of its rights simply because of its religious beliefs. . . .

I turn, next, to Justice SOUTER's second justification for finding an establishment of religion: his facile conclusion that the New York Legislature's creation of the Kiryas Joel School District was religiously motivated. But in the Land of the Free, democratically adopted laws are not so easily impeached by unelected judges. To establish the unconstitutionality of a facially neutral law on the mere basis of its asserted religiously preferential (or discriminatory) effects—or at least to establish it in conformity with our precedents—Justice SOUTER "must be able to show the absence of a neutral, secular basis" for the law. *Gillette v. United States*, 401 U. S. 437 (1971). . . .

Since the obvious presence of a neutral, secular basis renders the asserted preferential effect of this law inadequate to invalidate it, Justice SOUTER is required to come forward with direct evidence that religious preference was the objective. His case could scarcely be weaker. It consists, briefly, of this: The People of New York created the Kiryas Joel Village School District in order to further the Satmar religion, rather than for any proper secular purpose, because (1) they created the district in an extraordinary manner—by special Act of the legislature, rather than under the State's general laws governing school-district reorganization; (2) the creation of the district ran counter to a State trend towards consolidation of school districts; and (3) the District includes only adherents of the Satmar religion. On this indictment, no jury would convict.

One difficulty with the first point is that it is not true. There was really nothing so "special" about the formation of a school district by an Act of the New York Legislature. The State has created both large school districts, and small specialized school districts for institutionalized children, through these special Acts. But in any event all that the first point proves, and the second point as well (countering the trend toward consolidation), is that New York regarded Kiryas Joel as a special case, requiring special measures. I should think it obvious that it did, and obvious that it should have. But even if the New York Legislature had never before created a school district by special statute (which is not true), and even if it had done nothing but consolidate school districts for over a century (which is not true), how could the departure from those past practices possibly demonstrate that the legislature had religious favoritism in mind? It could not. To be sure, when there is no special treatment there is no possibility of religious favoritism; but it is not logical to suggest that when there is special treatment there is proof of religious favoritism.

Justice SOUTER's case against the statute comes down to nothing more, therefore, than his third point: the fact that all the residents of the Kiryas Joel Village School District are Satmars. But all its residents also wear unusual dress, have unusual civic customs, and have not much to do with people who are culturally different from them. (The Court recognizes that "the Satmars prefer to live together 'to facilitate individual religious observance and maintain social, cultural and religious values,' but that it is not 'against their religion' to interact with others." On what basis does Justice SOUTER conclude that it is the theological distinctiveness rather than the cultural distinctiveness that was the basis for New York State's decision? The normal assumption would be that it was the latter, since it was not theology but dress, language, and cultural alienation that posed the educational problem for the children. Justice SOUTER not only does not adopt the logical assumption, he does not even give the New York Legislature the benefit of the doubt. . . . In other words, we know the legislature must have been motivated by the desire to favor the Satmar Hasidim religion, because it could have met the needs of these children by a method that did not place the Satmar Hasidim in a separate school district. This is not a rational argument proving religious favoritism; it is rather a novel Establishment Clause principle to the effect that no secular objective may be pursued by a means that might also be used for religious favoritism if some other means is available. . . .

When a legislature acts to accommodate religion, particularly a minority sect, "it follows the best of our traditions." The Constitution itself contains an accommodation of sorts. Article VI, cl. 3, prescribes that executive, legislative and judicial officers of the Federal and State Governments shall bind themselves to support the Constitution "by Oath or Affirmation." Although members of the most populous religions found no difficulty in swearing an oath to God, Quakers, Moravians, and Mennonites refused to take oaths based on Matthew 5:34's injunction "swear not at all." The option of affirmation was added to accommodate these minority religions and enable their members to serve in government. Congress, from its earliest sessions, passed laws accommodating religion by refunding duties paid by specific churches upon the importation of plates for the printing of Bibles, vestments, and bells. Congress also exempted church property from the tax assessments it levied on residents of the District of Columbia; and all 50

States have had similar laws. . . .

In today's opinion, however, the Court seems uncomfortable with this aspect of our constitutional tradition. Although it acknowledges the concept of accommodation, it quickly points out that it is "not a principle without limits," and then gives reasons why the present case exceeds those limits, reasons which simply do not hold water. "We have never hinted," the Court says, "that an otherwise unconstitutional delegation of political power to a religious group could be saved as a religious accommodation." Putting aside the circularity inherent in referring to a delegation as "otherwise unconstitutional" when its constitutionality turns on whether there is an accommodation, if this statement is true, it is only because we have never hinted that delegation of political power to citizens who share a particular religion could be unconstitutional. This is simply a replay of the argument we rejected in Part II.

The second and last reason the Court finds accommodation impermissible is, astoundingly, the mere risk that the State will not offer accommodation to a similar group in the future, and that neutrality will therefore not be preserved. . . .

Contrary to the Court's suggestion, I do not think that the Establishment Clause prohibits formally established "state" churches and nothing more. I have always believed, and all my opinions are consistent with the view, that the Establishment Clause prohibits the favoring of one religion over others. In this respect, it is the Court that attacks lions of straw. What I attack is the Court's imposition of novel "up front" procedural requirements on state legislatures. Making law (and making exceptions) one case at a time, whether through adjudication or through highly particularized rulemaking or legislation, violates, *ex ante*, no principle of fairness, equal protection, or neutrality, simply because it does not announce in advance how all future cases (and all future exceptions) will be disposed of. If it did, the manner of proceeding of this Court itself would be unconstitutional. It is presumptuous for this Court to impose—out of nowhere—an unheard-of prohibition against proceeding in this manner upon the Legislature of New York State. I never heard of such a principle, nor has anyone else, nor will it ever be heard of again. Unlike what the New York Legislature has done, this is a special rule to govern only the Satmar Hasidim. . . .

Finally, Justice O'CONNOR observes that the Court's opinion does not focus on the so-called *Lemon* test, and she urges that that test be abandoned, at least as a "unitary approach" to all Establishment Clause claims. . . . Unlike Justice O'CONNOR, however, I would not replace *Lemon* with nothing, and let the case law "evolve" into a series of situation-specific rules (government speech on religious topics, government benefits to particular groups, etc.) unconstrained by any "rigid influence." The problem with (and the allure of) *Lemon* has not been that it is "rigid," but rather that in many applications it has been utterly meaningless, validating whatever result the Court would desire. To replace *Lemon* with nothing is simply to announce that we are now so bold that we no longer feel the need even to pretend that our haphazard course of Establishment Clause decisions is governed by any principle. The foremost principle I would apply is fidelity to the longstanding traditions of our people, which surely provide the diversity of treatment that Justice O'CONNOR seeks, but do not leave us to our own devices.

The Court's decision today is astounding. Chapter 748 involves no public aid to private schools and does not mention religion. In order to invalidate it, the Court casts aside, on the flimsiest of evidence, the strong presumption of validity that attaches to facially neutral laws, and invalidates the present accommodation because it does not trust New York to be as accommodating toward other religions (presumably those less powerful than the Satmar Hasidim) in the future. This is unprecedented—except that it continues, and takes to new extremes, a recent tendency in the opinions of this Court to turn the Establishment Clause into a repealer of our Nation's tradition of religious toleration. I dissent.

8

THE FIFTH AMENDMENT GUARANTEE AGAINST SELF-ACCUSATION

OVER THE YEARS the Court has handed down conflicting rulings on when a person is technically "in custody" and hence entitled to *Miranda* warnings and, in the absence of those warnings, entitled to have incriminating statements made during police questioning excluded as evidence at trial (see Vol. 2 Ch. 8). As a result, police have been generally given a freer hand in interrogating individuals. But, shortly after hearing oral arguments in *Stansbury v. California*, 114 S.Ct. 1526 (1994), the Supreme Court unanimously drew a line at lower courts' allowing police officers' subjective views, in contrast to objective factors, to determine when a person is "in custody" for the purposes of *Miranda*.

Mr. Stansbury had responded to a knock on his door by police, who were investigating a homicide, and agreed to accompany them to the police station for questioning. At the station, Stansbury was questioned about his activities, without being given his *Miranda* warnings, and said that he had last seen the victim about midnight when he had left the victim's trailer in his housemate's turquoise American-made car. That last detail aroused the police's suspicions, since a turquoise car had been identified as associated with the homicide. When Stansbury admitted, in repsonse to further questioning, that he had prior convictions for rape, kidnapping, and child molestation, the police terminated their questioning and advised Stansbury of his *Miranda* rights. Stansbury thereafter declined to answer further questions, requested an attorney, and was subsequently arrested and charged with first-degree murder. His attorney later filed a pre-trial motion to suppress all of the statements he had made at the station house. But, the trial court denied that motion on the ground that Stansbury was not "in custody" at the time of his questioning and therefore not entitled to *Miranda* warnings. The California state supreme court agreed and Stansbury appealed that ruling to the Supreme Court.

In a brief *per curiam* opinion reversing the state court's ruling, the Rehnquist Court held that,

> Our decisions make clear that the initial determination of custody depends on the objective circumstances of the interrogation, not on the subjective views harbored by either the interrogating officers or the person being questioned. In *Beckwith v. United States*, 425 U.S. 341 (1976), for example, the defendant, without being advised of his *Miranda* rights, made incriminating statements to Government agents during an interview in a private home. He later asked that *Miranda* "be extended to cover interrogation in non-custodial circumstances after a police investigation has focused on the suspect." We found his argument unpersuasive, explaining that it "was the complusive aspect of custodial interrogation, and not the strength or content of the government's suspicions at the time the questioning was conducted, which led the Court to impose *Miranda* requirements with regard to custodial questioning." As a result, we concluded that the defendant was not entitled to *Miranda* warnings . . . .
>
> It is well settled, then, that a police officer's subjective view that the individual under questioning is a suspect, if undisclosed, does not bear upon the question whether the individual is in custody for purposes of *Miranda*. The same principle obtains if an officer's undisclosed assessment is that the person being questioned is not a suspect. In either instance, one cannot expect the person under interrogation to probe the officer's innermost thoughts. Save as they are communicated or otherwise manifested to the person being questioned, an officer's evolving but unarticulated suspicions do not affect the objective circumstances of an interrogation or interview, and thus cannot affect the *Miranda* custody inquiry.

In another *Miranda*-related case, *Davis v. United States*, 114 S.Ct. — (1994), the Court was asked to clarify what constitutes a suspect's request for an attorney and whether police must stop their questioning at the suspect's request. Robert L. Davis, a Navy sailor who was accused of murdering a man who refused to pay off a pool wager, was handcuffed to a chair during an interrogation about his whereabouts at the time of the murder. At the outset of the interrogation, Davis was informed of his *Miranda* rights but said that he did not need a lawyer. Subsequently, when told that his girlfriend had contradicted his account of where he was the night of the murder, and reminded that he had earlier admitted winning thirty dollars in a pool game with the victim, Davis said, "Maybe I should talk to a lawyer." When the questioning continued and agents sought to clarify whether he really wanted a lawyer, Davis then again contradicted his earlier request. As a result, some incriminating statements made during his interrogation were used against him at trial, and the U.S. Court of Military Appeals held that the interrogation was proper and upheld the use of self-incriminating statements.

Writing for the Court, Justice O'Connor affirmed the lower court's ruling and held that Davis's statment was not a request for counsel and

Blackmun, Stevens, and Ginsburg joined Justice Souter's concurring opinion, which objected to O'Connor's suggestion that the police could have disregarded Davis's statement without seeking further clarification of whether he wanted an attorney.

that the officers were not required to seek further clarification of his statement (which they had in any event). In O'Connor's words:

> The right to counsel in *Miranda* is sufficiently important to suspects in criminal investigations, we have held, that it "requires the special protection of the knowing and intelligent waiver standard." *Edwards v. Arizona*, 451 U.S. [477 (1981)]. If the suspect effectively waives his right to counsel after receiving *Miranda* warnings, law enforcement officers are free to question him. *North Carolina v. Butler*, 441 U.S. 369 (1979). But if a suspect requests counsel at any time during the interview, he is not subject to further questioning until a lawyer has been made available or the suspect himself reinitiates conversation. This "second layer of prophylaxis for the *Miranda* right to counsel," *McNeil v. Wisconsin*, 501 U.S. 171 (1991), is "designed to prevent police from badgering a defendant into waiving his previously asserted *Miranda* rights," *Michigan v. Harvey*, 494 U.S. 344 (1990). To that end, we have held that a suspect who has invoked the right to counsel cannot be questioned regarding any offense unless an attorney is actually present. *Minnick v. Mississippi*, 498 U.S. 146 (1990); *Arizona v. Roberson*, 486 U.S. 675 (1988). "It makes clear, however, that this prohibition on further questioning-like other aspects of *Miranda*-is not required of the Fifth Amendment's prohibition on coerced confessions, but is instead justified only by reference to its prophylactic purpose." . . .
>
> We decline petitioner's invitation to extend *Edwards* and require law enforcement officiers to cease questioning immediately upon the making of an ambiguous or equivocal reference to an attorney. The rationale underlying *Edwards* is that the police must respect a suspect's wishes regarding his right to have an attorney present during custodial interrogation. But when the officers conducting the questioning reasonably do not know whether or not the suspect wants a lawyer, a rule requiring the immediate cessation of questioning "would transform the *Miranda* safeguards into wholly irrational obstacles to legitimate police investigative activity," *Michigan v. Mosley*, 423 U.S. 96 (1975), because it would needlessly prevent the police from questioning a suspect in the absence of counsel even if the suspect did not wish to have a lawyer present. Nothing in *Edwards* requires the provision of counsel to a suspect who consents to answer questions without the assistance of a lawyer. In *Miranda* itself, we expressly rejected the suggestion "that each police station must have a `station house lawyer' present at all times to advise prisoners," and held instead that a suspect must be told of his right to have an attorney present and that he may not be questioned after invoking his right to counsel. We also noted that if a suspect is "indecisive in his request for counsel," the officers need not always cease questioning.
>
> We recognize that requiring a clear assertion of the right to counsel might disadvantage some suspects who—because of fear, intimidation, lack of linguistic skills, or a variety of other reasons—will not clearly articulate their right to counsel although they actually want to have a lawyer present. But the primary protection afforded suspects subject to custodial interrogation is the *Miranda* warnings themselves.

Separate concurrances were filed by Justices Scalia and Souter. Justices

9

THE RIGHTS TO COUNSEL AND OTHER PROCEDURAL GUARANTEES

G. THE GUARANTEE AGAINST DOUBLE JEOPARDY

Over the last decade the Court has been reconsidering the scope of the Fifth Amendment's bar against being held in double jeopardy for the same offense, and thereby invited the litigation of such claims. In *Schiro v. Farley*, 114 S.Ct. 783 (1994), a majority of the Rehnquist Court declined an invitation to apply the double jeopardy clause to the sentencing stage of a capital case and on that basis to vacate Thomas Schiro's death sentence. Only dissenting Justices Blackmun and Stevens thought otherwise, as the latter explained:

> The jury found Thomas Schiro guilty of felony murder but not intentional murder. Thereafter, in a separate sentencing hearing, the same jury unanimously concluded that Schiro did not deserve the death penalty, presumably because he had not intended to kill. Nevertheless, without finding any aggravating circumstance, the trial judge overrode the jury's recommendation and sentenced Schiro to death. Months later, when the Indiana Supreme Court remanded the case to give the judge an opportunity to justify that sentence, the judge found that Schiro had intentionally killed his victim. That finding, like the majority's holding today, violated the central purpose of the Double Jeopardy Clause. After the issue of intent had been raised at trial and twice resolved by the jury, and long after that jury had been discharged, it was constitutionally impermissible for the trial judge to reexamine the issue. Because the death sentence rests entirely on that unauthorized finding, the law requires that it be set aside.
>
> The Court devotes most of its opinion to a discussion of the facts. I cannot disagree that the gruesome character of the crime is significant. It is important

> precisely because it is so favorable to prosecutors seeking the death penalty. Such facts undoubtedly would increase jurors' inclination to impose the death penalty if they believed the defendant had intentionally killed his unfortunate victim. Yet in this case, despite the horror of the crime, the jurors still unanimously refused to find Schiro guilty of intentional murder and unanimously concluded that he should not be executed. These determinations are enigmatic unless the jury resolved the intent issue in Schiro's favor.

By contrast, writing for the majority in *Schiro* Justice O'Connor observed that,

> Schiro urges us to treat the sentencing phase of a single prosecution as a successive prosecution for purposes of the Double Jeopardy Clause. We decline to do so. Our prior decisions are inconsistent with the argument that a first sentencing proceeding can amount to a successive prosecution. In *Stroud v. United States*, 251 U.S. 15 (1919), we held that where a defendant's murder conviction was overturned on appeal, the defendant could be resentenced after retrial. Similarly, we found no constitutional informity in holding a second sentencing hearing where the first sentence was improperly based on a prior conviction for which the defendant had been pardoned. *Lockhart v. Nelson*, 488 U.S. 33 (1988). If a second sentencing proceeding ordinarily does not violate the double jeopardy clause, we fail to see how an initial sentencing proceeding could do so.
>
> We have also upheld the use of prior convictions to enhance sentences for subsequent convictions, even though this means a defendant must, in a certain sense, relitigate in a sentencing proceedding conduct for which he was previously tried. *Spenser v. Texas*, 385 U.S. 554 (1967). In short, as applied to successive prosecutions, the Clause "is written in terms of potential or risk of trial and conviction, not punishment." *Pierce v. Georgia*, 398 U.S. 323 (1970).

In another ruling on the scope of the double jeopardy clause, the justices split five to four when striking down Montana's tax on illegal drugs in *Department of Revenue of Montana v. Kurth Ranch*, 114 S.Ct. — (1994). Along with more than twenty other states, Montana imposed a tax on illegal drugs confiscated in drug raids. Montana's statute assessed a tax of $100 per ounce on marijuana plants and defended it as a fund raising, not a punitive, measure. But, the tax was challenged for constituting a form of double jeopardy, since it imposed an additional penalty inflicted on those convicted of possessing illegal drugs and thus unconstitutionally punished people twice for the same offense. Writing for a bare majority, Justice Stevens rejected Montana's claim that its tax was simply a revenue-raising measure. "This tax, imposed on criminals and no others, departs so far from normal revenue laws as to become a form of punishment," said Justice Stevens, who further added that,

> As a general matter, the unlawfulness of an activity does not prevent its taxation.

> Montana, no doubt, could collect its tax on the possession of marijuana, for example, if it had not previously punished the taxpayer for the same offense, or, indeed, if it had assessed the tax in the same proceeding that resulted in his conviction. . . . [But] this drug tax is a concoction of anomalies, too far removed in crucial respects from a standard tax assessment to escape characterization as punishment for the purpose of double jeopardy analysis.

The four dissenters, however, took strong exception to Justice Stevens's analysis. Noting that a number of states had enacted similar laws in their "war on drugs," dissenting Justice O'Connor charged that the ruling "will be felt acutely by law-abiding taxpayers, because it will seriously undermine the ability of the state and federal governments to collect recompense for the immense costs criminals impose on our society." In a separate dissenting opinion, Chief Justice Rehnquist countered that Montana's tax was comparable to other valid "sin taxes," such as those imposed on alcohol and cigarettes, which aim at raising money and discouraging certain kinds of behavior. In a third dissenting opinion, joined by Justice Thomas, Justice Scalia dismissed flat out the majority's analysis. The Fifth Amendment's double jeopardy clause, he maintained, should apply only to successive prosecutions, not successive punishments.

10

CRUEL AND UNUSUAL PUNISHMENT

A. NONCAPITAL PUNISHMENT

While the Rehnquist Court was rather bitterly divided in rulings extending the scope of the Eighth Amendment's cruel and unusual punishment clause to conditions of imprisonment and the treatment of prisoners (see *Wilson v. Seiter*, 111 S.Ct. 2321 (1991), and *Hudson v. McMillian*, 112 S.Ct. 995 (1992), in Vol. 2, Ch. 10), the justices unanimously reinstated a suit for damages brought by a transsexual inmate in *Farmer v. Brennan*, 114 S.Ct. — (1994). Dee Farmer, who is serving a twenty-year sentence for credit card fraud, was born male but underwent estrogen therapy, had breast implants, and had unsuccessful surgery to remove his testicles. In prison, Farmer was raped and subsequently claimed that prison officials should not have put him with the general prison population because they should have known that a transsexual "who projects feminine characteristics" would be vulnerable to sexual assaults.

In holding for the Court that Farmer could sue for damages based on showing that prison officials exhibited "deliberate indifference" to his safety, Justice Souter observed that, "Being violently assaulted in prison is simply not part of the penalty that criminal offenders pay for their offenses against society." Although concurring in the judgment in a separate opinion, Justice Thomas maintained his position that the Eighth Amendment does not extend to brutality among prisoners or inflicted by guards. As Justice Thomas put it, "Punishment, from the time of the founding through the present day, has always meant a fine, penalty or confinement inflicted upon a person by the authority of the law and the judgment and sentence of a court, for some crime or offense committed by him. . . . Because the unfortunate attack that befell petitioner was not part of his sentence, it did not constitute 'punishment' under the Eighth Amendment."

B. CAPITAL PUNISHMENT

Although the Rehnquist Court has made it easier to impose death sentences and has expedited the carrying out of capital punishment (see Vol. 2, Ch. 10), it continues to review numerous death penalty appeals each year. See "The Development of Law" box in this chapter. Among the death penalty appeals granted and decided in the 1993-1994 term, two leading cases were *Tuilaepa v. California* and *Proctor v. California*, 114 S.Ct. — (1994). Both challenged California's system for imposing capital punishment. Under that state's law, juries are instructed during the sentencing stage of capital murder trials to consider all relevant aspects of defendant's character, crime, and record. Attorneys appealing the death sentences of two convicted murderers argued that California's law was constitutionally inadequate because it failed to specify the aggravating and mitigating factors that juries should weigh when deciding on whether to impose a death sentence. Until the watershed 1972 ruling in *Furman v. Georgia* (in Vol. 2, Ch. 10), there were no national standards for imposing death sentences. *Furman* struck down the then-existing death penalty statutes for failing to provide adequate jury instructions and for inviting arbitrary and capricious decisions. Subsequently, the Court upheld death penalty statutes that specified the aggravating factors that juries should consider and on which to base death sentences. Jury discretion with respect to mitigating factors, such as the defendant's youth, however, was held not to be limited to only those factors spelled out in a statute.

Not until the last day of its term, June 30, 1994, did the Court hand down its decision in *Tuilaepa* and *Proctor*. Then, by a vote of eight to one, the Court upheld California's jury instructions in death penalty cases. Writing for the majority, Justice Kennedy held that the factors in question were not unconstitutionally vague. Only Justice Blackmun dissented.

Prior to the Court's ruling in *Tuilaepa* and *Proctor*, Justice Blackmun handed down a dissent from the Court's denial of *certiorari* in *Callins v. Collins*, 114 S.Ct. 1127 (1994), explaining that he no longer believed that capital punishment was constitutional because there was no way to ensure against the arbitrary and capricious imposition of death sentences. In a lengthy opinion, Blackmun reviewed the Court's prior rulings and explained his switch in position on the imposition of capital punishment:

> Twenty years have passed since this Court declared that the death penalty must be imposed fairly, and with reasonable consistency, or not at all, see *Furman v. Georgia*, 408 U.S. 238 (1972), and, despite the effort of the States and courts to devise legal formulas and procedural rules to meet this daunting challenge, the death penalty remains fraught with arbitrariness, discrimination, caprice, and mistake. . . . Experience has taught us that the constitutional goal of eliminating arbitrariness and discrimination from the administration of death can never be achieved without compromising an equally essential component

of fundamental fairness—individualized sentencing. See *Lockett v. Ohio*, 438 U.S. 586 (1978). . . .

On their face, these goals of individual fairness, reasonable consistency, and absence of error appear to be attainable: Courts are in the very business of erecting procedural devices from which fair, equitable, and reliable outcomes are presumed to flow. Yet, in the death penalty area, this Court, in my view, has engaged in a futile effort to balance these constitutional demands, and now is retreating not only from the *Furman* promise of consistency and rationality, but from the requirement of individualized sentencing as well. . . .

From this day forward, I no longer shall tinker with the machinery of death. For more than 20 years I have endeavored—indeed, I have struggled—along with a majority of this Court, to develop procedural and substantive rules that would lend more than the mere appearance of fairness to the death penalty endeavor. Rather than continue to coddle the Court's delusion that the desired level of fairness has been achieved and the need for regulation eviscerated, I feel morally and intellectually obligated simply to concede that the death penalty experiment has failed. It is virtually self-evident to me now that no combination of procedural rules or substantive regulations ever can save the death penalty from its inherent constitutional deficiencies. The basic question—does the system accurately and consistently determine which defendants "deserve" to die?—cannot be answered in the affirmative. It is not simply that this Court has allowed vague aggravating circumstances to be employed. The problem is that the inevitability of factual, legal, and moral error gives us a system that we know must wrongly kill some defendants, a system that fails to deliver the fair, consistent, and reliable sentences of death required by the Constitution. . . .

There is a heightened need for fairness in the administration of death. This unique level of fairness is born of the appreciation that death truly is different from all other punishments a society inflicts upon its citizens. *Woodson [v. North Carolina*, 428 U.S. 280 (1976)].

The Court elaborated on the principle of individualized sentencing in *Lockett v. Ohio*, 438 U.S. 586 (1978). In that case, a plurality acknowledged that strict restraints on sentencer discretion are necessary to achieve the consistency and rationality promised in *Furman*, but held that, in the end, the sentencer must retain unbridled discretion to afford mercy. . . . I believe the *Woodson-Lockett* line of cases to be fundamentally sound and rooted in American standards of decency that have evolved over time. . . . Yet, as several Members of the Court have recognized, there is real "tension" between the need for fairness to the individual and the consistency promised in *Furman*.

[The] dilemma was laid bare in *Penry v. Lynaugh*, 492 U.S. 302 (1989). The defendant in *Penry* challenged the Texas death penalty statute, arguing that it failed to allow the sentencing jury to give full mitigating effect to his evidence of mental retardation and history of child abuse. The Texas statute required the jury, during the penalty phase, to answer three "special issues"; if the jury unanimously answered "yes" to each issue, the trial court was obligated to sentence the defendant to death. Only one of the three issues—whether the defendant posed a "continuing threat to society"—was related to the evidence Penry offered in mitigation. But Penry's evidence of mental retardation and child abuse was a two-edged sword as it related to that special issue: "it diminished his blameworthiness for his crime even as it indicated that there

[was] a probability that he [would] be dangerous in the future." The Court therefore reversed Penry's death sentence, explaining that a reasonable juror could have believed that the statute prohibited a sentence less than death based upon his mitigating evidence. . . .

The theory underlying *Penry* and *Lockett* is that an appropriate balance can be struck between the *Furman* promise of consistency and the *Lockett* requirement of individualized sentencing if the death penalty is conceptualized as consisting of two distinct stages. In the first stage of capital sentencing, the demands of *Furman* are met by "narrowing" the class of death-eligible offenders according to objective, fact-bound characteristics of the defendant or the circumstances of the offense. Once the pool of death-eligible defendants has been reduced, the sentencer retains the discretion to consider whatever relevant mitigating evidence the defendant chooses to offer.

Over time, I have come to conclude that even this approach is unacceptable: It simply reduces, rather than eliminates, the number of people subject to arbitrary sentencing. It is the decision to sentence a defendant to death—not merely the decision to make a defendant eligible for death—that may not be arbitrary. While one might hope that providing the sentencer with as much relevant mitigating evidence as possible will lead to more rational and consistent sentences, experience has taught otherwise. It seems that the decision whether a human being should live or die is so inherently subjective—rife with all of life's understandings, experiences, prejudices, and passions—that it inevitably defies the rationality and consistency required by the Constitution.

The arbitrariness inherent in the sentencer's discretion to afford mercy is exacerbated by the problem of race. . . . A renowned example of racism infecting a capital-sentencing scheme is documented in *McCleskey v. Kemp*, 481 U.S. 279 (1987). Warren McCleskey, an African-American, argued that the Georgia capital-sentencing scheme was administered in a racially discriminatory manner, in violation of the Eighth and Fourteenth Amendments. . . .

In apparent frustration over its inability to strike an appropriate balance between the *Furman* promise of consistency and the *Lockett* requirement of individualized sentencing, the Court has retreated from the field, allowing relevant mitigating evidence to be discarded, vague aggravating circumstances to be employed, and providing no indication that the problem of race in the administration of death will ever be addressed. . . . In my view, the proper course when faced with irreconcilable constitutional commands is not to ignore one or the other, nor to pretend that the dilemma does not exist, but to admit the futility of the effort to harmonize them. This means accepting the fact that the death penalty cannot be administered in accord with our Constitution. . . .

In a concurring opinion to the denial of *certiorari* in *Callins v. Collins*, Justice Scalia responded to Blackmun's turn-about and analysis, observing that,

Convictions in opposition to the death penalty are often passionate and deeply held. That would be no excuse for reading them into a Constitution that does not contain them, even if they represented the convictions of a majority of Americans. Much less is there any excuse for using that course to thrust a

> minority's views upon the people. Justice BLACKMUN begins his statement by describing with poignancy the death of a convicted murderer by lethal injection. He chooses, as the case in which to make that statement, one of the less brutal of the murders that regularly come before us—the murder of a man ripped by a bullet suddenly and unexpectedly, with no opportunity to prepare himself and his affairs, and left to bleed to death on the floor of a tavern. The death-by-injection which Justice BLACKMUN describes looks pretty desirable next to that. It looks even better next to some of the other cases currently before us which Justice BLACKMUN did not select as the vehicle for his announcement that the death penalty is always unconstitutional—for example, the case of the 11-year-old girl raped by four men and then killed by stuffing her panties down her throat. See *McCollum v. North Carolina, cert.* now pending before the Court. How enviable a quiet death by lethal injection compared with that! If the people conclude that such more brutal deaths may be deterred by capital punishment; indeed, if they merely conclude that justice requires such brutal deaths to be avenged by capital punishment; the creation of false, untextual and unhistorical contradictions within "the Court's Eighth Amendment jurisprudence" should not prevent them.

In its 1994-1995 term the Court will decide whether the standard set forth in *Brecht v. Abrahamson*, 113 S.Ct. 1710 (1993), for federal review of *habeas corpus* petitions should apply to appeals in capital cases. In *Brecht*, a bare majority ruled that *habeas* petitioners must prove that constitutional errors during a state trial "had a substantial and injurious effect or influence in determining the jury's verdict," and therefore merit federal courts' review. Here, a death row inmate claims that he was denied a fair trial both because prosecutors wrongly withheld evidence that would have cleared him and because his attorney gave him inadequate assistance. The Court of Appeals for the Fifth Circuit rejected his claims that the trial errors were so serious as to deprive him of a fair trial and the inmate appealed that ruling in *Kyles v. Whitley*.

THE DEVELOPMENT OF LAW

Other Recent Rulings of the Rehnquist Court on Capital Punishment

Case	Vote	Ruling
Schiro v. Farley, 114 S.Ct. 783 (1994)	7:2	Rejected a double jeopardy challenge to a death sentence and claim that the double jeopardy clause applies to the sentencing stage of a capital murder trial. Justices Blackmun and Stevens dissented.
Romano v. Oklahoma, 114 S.Ct. – (1994)	5:4	Commanding a bare majority, Chief Justice Rehnquist held that the introduction as evidence in a capital trial of the judgment and death sentence in an earlier trial for another murder does not violate the Eighth Amendment or infect the sentencing determination and balancing of aggravating and mitigating factors when imposing a second death sentence. Justices Blackmun, Ginsburg, Stevens, and Souter dissented.
Simmons v. South Carolina, 114 S. Ct. – (1994)	7:2	Writing for a plurality of the Court, Justice Blackmun held that during the sentencing stage of a capital trial, if the prosecution argues that the accused's future dangerousness is a factor to be considered by the jury in determining whether to impose a death sentence or life imprisonment, then due process requires that the jury also be instructed that the accused is ineligible for parole under state law. In a separate opinion, joined by Chief Justice Rehnquist and Justice Kennedy, Justice O'Connor concluded that due process requires a jury to be instructed of an accused's parole ineligibility *only if* the prosecution makes an issue of the defendant's future dangerousness at the sentencing stage of a murder trial. Justices Scalia and Thomas dissented.
Tuilaepa v. California, 114 S.Ct. — (1994)	8:1	Writing for the Court, Justice Kennedy held that California's instructions for juries when determining whether to impose a death sentence were not unconstitutionally vague. The provisions challenged provided that juries consider, among other factors, the "circumstances of the crime of which the defendant was convicted . . . and the existence of any special circumstances found to be true," and the "presence or absence of criminal activity (involving) the use or attempted use of force or violence or the express or implied threat to use force or violence," as well as the defendant's age at the time of the crime. Justice Blackmun dissented.

11

THE RIGHT OF PRIVACY

A. PRIVACY AND REPRODUCTIVE FREEDOM

The Court is now entering a second generation of litigation stemming from the controversy over abortion that was sparked by the landmark ruling in *Roe v. Wade*, 410 U.S. 113 (1973) (see Vol. 2, Ch. 11). In the wake of the Rehnquist Court's controversial abortion ruling in *Planned Parenthood of Southeastern Pennsylvania v. Casey*, 112 S.Ct. 2791 (1992) (see Vol. 2, Ch. 11), lower courts have become split in applying *Casey*'s "undue burden" test to restrictive abortion laws. Yet, the Court has refused to clarify its analysis and declined to grant a number of appeals of lower court rulings striking down or upholding restrictions on women seeking abortions. By a six-to-three vote and without explanation, the Court denied review of *Ada v. Guam Society of Obstetricians & Gynecologists*, 113 S.Ct. 633 (1992), in which the governor of the Territory of Guam appealed the Ninth Circuit's invalidation of Guam's 1990 law banning virtually all abortions. The Court also denied review of *Edwards v. Sojourner T.*, 113 S.Ct. 1414 (1993), which appealed the Eleventh Circuit's striking down Louisiana's 1991 ban on all abortions, except those necessary to save a woman's life and in cases of rape or incest. While those lower court rulings striking down very restrictive abortion laws were left standing, the Court also denied review of appeals of the Fifth Circuit's upholding provisions of Mississippi's anti-abortion law. By denying review in *Barnes v. Moore*, 113 S.Ct. 656 (1992), the Court left undisturbed the appellate court's analysis that under *Casey* Mississippi could require women seeking an abortion to wait twenty-four hours after giving their informed consent and having their doctors explain the medical risks of abortion, describe the stage of fetal development, as well as discuss pregnancy prevention and alternatives to abortion, along with notifying them "that the father is liable to assist in the support of her child." Mississippi's requirement that unmarried women under the age of eighteen obtain both of their parents' permission before having an abortion was also upheld by the Fifth Circuit, and the Court declined to review that decision, in *Barnes v. Mississippi*, 114 S.Ct. 468 (1993), as well. Mississippi's parental consent requirement (like those in Massachusetts, North Dakota, and other states that have been upheld), however, permits an unmarried teenager in extraordinary circumstances to obtain a judge's permission to obtain an abortion if she demonstrates maturity and it is not in her best interest to tell her parents about her desire to have an abortion.

There remains little doubt, though, the Court will revisit the controversy over *Casey's* undue burden test in its 1994 or 1995 term, particularly since the balance on the Court shifted with Justice Ginsburg's filling the seat of Justice White, who had dissented in *Roe* and sided with the minority in *Casey*. Almost two years after *Casey* upheld Pennsylvania's restrictions on abortion, and during which time there remained a lower court's stay on the enforcement of those restrictions, Justice Souter refused to grant a further stay. He did so in his capacity as the justice assigned to handle matters coming from the court of appeals for the Third Circuit, in a rather extraordinary six-page opinion in *Planned Parenthood of Southeastern Pennsylvania v. Casey*, 112 S.Ct. 2791 (1992). At issue remains the contention of abortion clinics that informed consent and twenty-four-hour waiting period requirements, even though upheld in *Casey*, may operate to create an undue burden for women who must take time off from work and who have to travel great distances to an abortion clinic. That argument was accepted by the court of appeals for the Eighth Circuit in 1993, when it barred North Dakota's twenty-four-hour waiting period requirement from taking effect because of the burdens it imposed on women seeking abortions at the state's sole abortion clinic in Fargo, North Dakota. Justice Souter cited approvingly that ruling and noted that, "The letter of our *Casey* opinion is not entirely hard-edged." Moreover, Justice Souter emphasized that, "Litigants are free to challenge similar restrictions in other jurisdictions." Inexorably, in the coming terms the Court will face the issues of (1) whether similar restrictions, such as twenty-four-hour waiting period requirements in different states fail to satisfy *Casey's* undue-burden test; and (2) whether restrictions, though permissible on their face, operate in such a way as to place undue burdens on women and are thus unconstitutional.

Other cases stemming from the controversy over abortion revolve around attempts to bring lawsuits against anti-abortion protesters and demonstrators, who have intimidated women, blockaded abortion clincs, and even engaged in fire bombings and shootings of doctors. In *Bray v. Alexandria Women's Health Clinic*, 113 S.Ct. 753 (1993) (in Vol. 2, Ch. 11), the Rehnquist Court was bitterly split five to four in holding that the Civil Rights Act of 1871 does not give federal judges jurisdiction to enjoin the activities of anti-abortion protesters. However, in *National Organization for Women v. Scheidler*, 114 S.Ct. 798 (1994) (see below), the Court unanimously agreed that anti-abortion protesters could be sued for conspiracy and damages under the Racketeer Influenced and Corrupt Organizations (RICO) Act. Notably, though, in a concurring opinion joined by Justice Kennedy, Justice Souter indicated that the ruling in *Scheidler* did not preclude further consideration of the First Amendment claims of anti-abortion protesters.

In the same week that *Scheidler* came down, the justices also announced that they would finally grant review of a case involving anti-abortion protesters' claims of the First Amendment when fighting restrictions imposed on their protests and demonstrations. Courts throughout the country had been divided on that issue, raised in *Madsen v. Women's Health Center*, 114 S.Ct. — (1994). *Madsen* is excerpted in Chapter 5.

National Organization for Women v. Scheidler

114 S.Ct. 798 (1994)

Confronted with an increasing number and increasingly violent anti-abortion protests at abortion clinics around the country, the National Organization for Women (NOW), the Delaware Women's Health Organization, and the Summit Women's Health Organization filed a suit in federal court against a number of leaders and organizations involved in anti-abortion protests. They did so under the Racketeer Influenced and Corrupt Organizations (RICO) Act, which prohibits any individual associated with an enterprise from engaging in racketeering activities. NOW and the other petitioners alleged that the anti-abortion protesters were members of a nationwide conspiracy to shut down abortion clinics through a pattern of racketeering activity, including extortion. Under federal law, extortion is defined as "the obtaining of property from another, with his consent, induced by wrongful use of the actual or threatened force, violence, or fear, or under color of official right." NOW argued that the anti-abortion protesters conspired to use threatened or actual force, violence and fear to induce clinic employees, doctors, and patients to give up their jobs, give up their economic right to practice medicine, and give up their right to obtain medical services at clinics. NOW also argued that anti-abortion organizations received income from supporters and made them subject to the provisions of the RICO Act. A federal district court, however, dismissed NOW's RICO claim on the ground that the income of the anti-abortion groups came from voluntary donations and "in no way were derived from the pattern of racketeering alleged in the complaint." That decision was affirmed by a federal appellate court and NOW appealed to the Supreme Court, which granted review.

The Court's decision was unanimous and the opinion was written by Chief Justice Rehnquist. Justice Souter filed a concurring opinion, joined by Justice Kennedy.

Chief Justice REHNQUIST delivered the opinion of the Court.

[The question presented here is] whether the racketeering enterprise or the racketeering predicate acts must be accompanied by an underlying economic motive. Section 1962(c) makes it unlawful "for any person employed by or associated with any enterprise engaged in, or the activities of which affect, interstate or foreign commerce, to conduct or participate, directly or indirectly, in the conduct of such enterprise's affairs through a pattern of racketeering activity or collection of unlawful debt." Section 1961(1) defines "pattern of racketeering activity" to include conduct that is "chargeable" or "indictable" under a host of state and federal laws. RICO broadly defines "enterprise" in Section 1961(4) to "include any individual, partnership, corporation, association, or other legal entity, and any union or group of individuals associated in fact although not a legal entity." Nowhere in either Section 1962(c), or in the RICO definitions in Section 1961, is there any indication that an economic motive is required.

The phrase "any enterprise engaged in, or the activities of which affect, interstate or foreign commerce" comes the closest of any language in subsection (c) to suggesting a need for an economic motive. Arguably an enterprise engaged in interstate or foreign commerce would have a profit-seeking motive, but the language in Section 1962(c) does not stop there; it includes enterprises whose activities "affect" interstate or foreign commerce. *Webster's Third New International Dictionary* (1969) defines "affect" as "to have a detrimental influence on-used especially in the phrase affecting commerce." An enterprise surely can have a detrimental influence on interstate or foreign commerce without having its own profit-seeking motives.

We do not believe that the usage of the term "enterprise" in subsections (a) and (b) leads to the inference that an economic motive is required in subsection (c). . . . [T]he "enterprise" in subsection (c) connotes generally the vehicle through which the unlawful pattern of racketeering activity is committed, rather than the victim of that activity. Subsection (c) makes it unlawful for "any person employed by or associated with any enterprise . . . to conduct or participate . . . in the conduct of such enterprise's affairs through a pattern of racketeering activity. . . ." Consequently, since the enterprise in subsection (c) is not being acquired, it need not have a property interest that can be acquired nor an economic motive for engaging in illegal activity; it need only be an association in fact that engages in a pattern of racketeering activity. . . .

Congress has not, either in the definitional section or in the operative language, required that an "enterprise" in Section 1962(c) have an economic motive. . . .

Both parties rely on legislative history to support their positions. We believe the statutory language is unambiguous, and find in the parties' submissions respecting legislative history no such "clearly expressed legislative intent to the contrary" that would warrant a different construction. Respondents finally argue that the result here should be controlled by the rule of lenity in criminal cases. But the rule of lenity applies only when an ambiguity is present. . . . We simply do not think there is an ambiguity here which would suffice to invoke the rule of lenity. "The fact that RICO has been applied in situations not expressly anticipated by Congress does not demonstrate ambiguity. It demonstrates breadth." *Sedima, S.P.R.L. v. Imrex, Co.*, 473 U.S. 479 (1985).

We therefore hold that petitioners may maintain this action if respondents conducted the enterprise through a pattern of racketeering activity. The questions of whether the respondents committed the requisite predicate acts, and whether the commission of these acts fell into a pattern, are not before us. We hold only that RICO contains no economic motive requirement.

Justice SOUTER, with whom Justice KENNEDY joins, concurring.

I join the Court's opinion and write separately to explain [that] the First Amendment does not require reading an economic-motive requirement into the RICO, and to stress that the Court's opinion does not bar First Amendment challenges to RICO's application in particular cases. . . .

12

EQUAL PROTECTION OF THE LAWS

D. NONRACIAL CLASSIFICATIONS AND THE EQUAL PROTECTION OF THE LAWS

(1) Gender-based Discrimination

In a sweeping and unanimous decision, in *Harris v. Forklift Systems, Inc.*, 114 S.Ct. 367 (1993), that will make it easier for individuals to prove sexual harassment in the workplace, the Supreme Court held that under Title VII of the Civil Rights Act of 1964, individuals need not meet the high standard of proving "psychological injury." In *Meritor Savings Bank v. Vinson*, 477 U.S. 57 (1986) (see Vol. 2, Ch. 12), the Court held that the Civil Rights Act forbids harassment in the workplace, along with discrimination in the hiring and firing of employees. But, lower courts were divided over the standards for proving harassment. Writing for the Court, Justice O'Connor explained that judges and juries have substantial leeway to decide whether sexual advances, insults, and other discriminatory conduct constitute harassment. In Justice O'Connor's words:

> Title VII of the Civil Rights Act of 1964 makes it "an unlawful employment practice for an employer . . . to discriminate against any individual with respect to his compensation, terms, conditions, or privileges of employment, because of such individual's race, color, religion, sex, or national origin." As we made clear in *Meritor Savings Bank v. Vinson*, 477 U.S. 57 (1986), this language "is not limited to 'economic' or 'tangible' discrimination. The phrase 'terms, conditions, or privileges of employment' evinces a congressional intent 'to strike at the entire spectrum of disparate treatment of men and women' in employment," which includes requiring people to work in a discriminatorily hostile or abusive

environment. When the workplace is permeated with "discriminatory intimidation, ridicule, and insult," that is "sufficiently severe or pervasive to alter the conditions of the victim's employment and create an abusive working environment," Title VII is violated.

This standard, which we reaffirm today, takes a middle path between making actionable any conduct that is merely offensive and requiring the conduct to cause a tangible psychological injury. . . . But Title VII comes into play before the harassing conduct leads to a nervous breakdown. A discriminatorily abusive work environment, even one that does not seriously affect employees' psychological well-being, can and often will detract from employees' job performance, discourage employees from remaining on the job, or keep them from advancing in their careers. Moreover, even without regard to these tangible effects, the very fact that the discriminatory conduct was so severe or pervasive that it created a work environment abusive to employees because of their race, gender, religion, or national origin offends Title VII's broad rule of workplace equality. The appalling conduct alleged in *Meritor*, and the reference in that case to environments "'so heavily polluted with discrimination as to destroy completely the emotional and psychological stability of minority group workers,'" merely present some especially egregious examples of harassment. They do not mark the boundary of what is actionable. . . .

Title VII bars conduct that would seriously affect a reasonable person's psychological well-being, but the statute is not limited to such conduct. So long as the environment would reasonably be perceived, and is perceived, as hostile or abusive, *Meritor*, *supra*, there is no need for it also to be psychologically injurious.

This is not, and by its nature cannot be, a mathematically precise test. We need not answer today all the potential questions it raises, nor specifically address the EEOC's new regulations on this subject. But we can say that whether an environment is "hostile" or "abusive" can be determined only by looking at all the circumstances. These may include the frequency of the discriminatory conduct; its severity; whether it is physically threatening or humiliating, or a mere offensive utterance; and whether it unreasonably interferes with an employee's work performance. The effect on the employee's psychological well-being is, of course, relevant to determining whether the plaintiff actually found the environment abusive. But while psychological harm, like any other relevant factor, may be taken into account, no single factor is required.

In another important ruling, the Court split six to three in *J. E. B. v. Alabama ex rel. T. B.*, 114 S.Ct. 1419 (1994) (see below), when extending its earlier rulings barring the exclusion of jurors from serving on juries on the basis of race to gender discrimination in jury selection. Writing for the majority, Justice Blackmun held that such gender discrimination violates the Fourteenth Amendment and requires "heightened judicial scrutiny," while dissenting Chief Justice Rehnquist and Justices Scalia and Thomas sharply disagreed.

J. E. B. v. Alabama ex rel. T. B.

114 S.Ct. 1419 (1994)

James E. Bowman (J. E. B.) was put on trial for paternity and child support. Prior to the trial, the court assembled a panel of thirty-six jurors, twelve men and twenty-four females. After the trial judge excused three for cause, the prosecution used nine of its ten peremptory challenges to remove male jurors, while J. E. B.'s attorney used all but one of his strikes to remove female jurors. As a result, the jury was female and J. E. B.'s attorney objected to the prosecution's use of its peremptory challenges to strike male jurors as a violation of the Fourteenth Amendment's equal protection clause. Subsequently, the jury found J. E. B. to be the father, and the court ordered him to make child-support payments, as well as reaffirmed its decision that the Fourteenth Amendment does not bar gender-based peremptory challenges. A state appellate court affirmed, and the state supreme court denied review. J. E. B. in turn appealed to the U.S. Supreme Court, which granted review.

The Court's decision was six to three, and the majority's opinion was announced by Justice Blackmun. Justices Kennedy and O'Connor filed concurring opinions. Chief Justice Rehnquist and Justice Scalia filed dissenting opinions, which Justice Thomas joined.

Justice BLACKMUN delivered the opinion of the Court.

In *Batson v. Kentucky*, 476 U.S. 79 (1986), this Court held that the Equal Protection Clause of the Fourteenth Amendment governs the exercise of peremptory challenges by a prosecutor in a criminal trial. The Court explained that although a defendant has "no right to a 'petit jury composed in whole or in part of persons of his own race,'" quoting *Strauder v. West Virginia*, 100 U.S. 303 (1880), the "defendant does have the right to be tried by a jury whose members are selected pursuant to nondiscriminatory criteria." Since *Batson*, we have reaffirmed repeatedly our commitment to jury selection procedures that are fair and nondiscriminatory. We have recognized that whether the trial is criminal or civil, potential jurors, as well as litigants, have an equal protection right to jury selection procedures that are free from state-sponsored group stereotypes rooted in, and reflective of, historical prejudice. See *Powers v. Ohio*, 499 U.S. 400 (1991); *Edmonson v. Leesville Concrete Co.*, 500 U.S. 614 (1991); *Georgia v. McCollum*, 505 U.S. — (1992).

Today we are faced with the question of whether the Equal Protection Clause forbids intentional discrimination on the basis of gender, just as it prohibits discrimination on the basis of race. We hold that gender, like race, is an unconstitutional proxy for juror competence and impartiality. . . .

Discrimination on the basis of gender in the exercise of peremptory challenges is a relatively recent phenomenon. Gender-based peremptory strikes were hardly practicable for most of our country's existence, since, until the 19th century, women were completely excluded from jury service. . . .

Many States continued to exclude women from jury service well into the present century, despite the fact that women attained suffrage upon ratification of the Nineteenth Amendment in 1920. . . . In *Hoyt v. Florida*, 368 U.S. [57 (1961)], the Court found it reasonable, "despite the enlightened emancipation of women," to exempt women from mandatory jury service by statute, allowing women to serve on juries only if they volunteered to serve. The Court justified the differential exemption policy on the ground that women, unlike men, occupied a unique position "as the center of home and family life."

In 1975, the Court finally repudiated the reasoning of Hoyt and struck down, under the Sixth Amendment, an affirmative registration statute nearly identical to the one at issue in *Hoyt*. See *Taylor v. Louisiana*, 419 U.S. 522 (1975). . . . *Taylor* relied on Sixth Amendment principles, but the opinion's approach is consistent with the heightened equal protection scrutiny afforded gender-based classifications. Since *Reed v. Reed*, 404 U.S. 71 (1971), this Court consistently has subjected gender-based classifications to heightened scrutiny in recognition of the real danger that government policies that professedly are based on reasonable considerations in fact may be reflective of "archaic and overbroad" generalizations about gender, see *Schlesinger v. Ballard*, 419 U.S. 498 (1975), or based on "outdated misconceptions concerning the role of females in the home rather than in the 'marketplace and world of ideas.'" *Craig v. Boren*, 429 U.S. 190 (1976).

Despite the heightened scrutiny afforded distinctions based on gender, respondent argues that gender discrimination in the selection of the petit jury should be permitted, though discrimination on the basis of race is not. Respondent suggests that "gender discrimination in this country . . . has never reached the level of discrimination" against African-Americans, and therefore gender discrimination, unlike racial discrimination, is tolerable in the courtroom.

While the prejudicial attitudes toward women in this country have not been identical to those held toward racial minorities, the similarities between the experiences of racial minorities and women, in some contexts, "overpower those differences." . . . Certainly, with respect to jury service, African-Americans and women share a history of total exclusion, a history which came to an end for women many years after the embarrassing chapter in our history came to an end for African-Americans. . . .

Discrimination in jury selection, whether based on race or on gender, causes harm to the litigants, the community, and the individual jurors who are wrongfully excluded from participation in the judicial process. The litigants are harmed by the risk that the prejudice which motivated the discriminatory selection of the jury will infect the entire proceedings. The community is harmed by the State's participation in the perpetuation of invidious group stereotypes and the inevitable loss of confidence in our judicial system that state-sanctioned discrimination in the courtroom engenders. . . .

Our conclusion that litigants may not strike potential jurors solely on the basis of gender does not imply the elimination of all peremptory challenges.

Neither does it conflict with a State's legitimate interest in using such challenges in its effort to secure a fair and impartial jury. Parties still may remove jurors whom they feel might be less acceptable than others on the panel; gender simply may not serve as a proxy for bias. Parties may also exercise their peremptory challenges to remove from the venire any group or class of individuals normally subject to "rational basis" review. Even strikes based on characteristics that are disproportionately associated with one gender could be appropriate, absent a showing of pretext. . . .

Equal opportunity to participate in the fair administration of justice is fundamental to our democratic system. It not only furthers the goals of the jury system. It reaffirms the promise of equality under the law—that all citizens, regardless of race, ethnicity, or gender, have the chance to take part directly in our democracy. When persons are excluded from participation in our democratic processes solely because of race or gender, this promise of equality dims, and the integrity of our judicial system is jeopardized. . . .

The judgment of the Court of Civil Appeals of Alabama is reversed and the case is remanded to that court for further proceedings not inconsistent with this opinion.

Justice O'CONNOR, concurring.

I write separately to discuss some of these costs, and to express my belief that today's holding should be limited to the government's use of gender-based peremptory strikes. . . .

I adhere to my position that the Equal Protection Clause does not limit the exercise of peremptory challenges by private civil litigants and criminal defendants. This case itself presents no state action dilemma, for here the State of Alabama itself filed the paternity suit on behalf of petitioner. But what of the next case? Will we, in the name of fighting gender discrimination, hold that the battered wife—on trial for wounding her abusive husband—is a state actor? Will we preclude her from using her peremptory challenges to ensure that the jury of her peers contains as many women members as possible? I assume we will, but I hope we will not.

Justice SCALIA, with whom the CHIEF JUSTICE and Justice THOMAS join, dissenting.

Today's opinion is an inspiring demonstration of how thoroughly up-to-date and right-thinking we Justices are in matters pertaining to the sexes (or as the Court would have it, the genders), and how sternly we disapprove the male chauvinist attitudes of our predecessors. The price to be paid for this display—a modest price, surely—is that most of the opinion is quite irrelevant to the case at hand. The hasty reader will be surprised to learn, for example, that this lawsuit involves a complaint about the use of peremptory challenges to exclude men from a petit jury. To be sure, petitioner, a man, used all but one of his peremptory strikes to remove women from the jury (he used his last challenge to strike the sole remaining male from the pool), but the validity of his strikes is not before us. Nonetheless, the Court treats itself to an extended discussion of the historic exclusion of women not only from jury service, but also from service at the bar (which is rather like jury service, in that it involves going to the courthouse a lot). All this, as I say, is irrelevant, since the case involves state action that allegedly discriminates against men. . . .

Although the Court's legal reasoning in this case is largely obscured by anti-male-chauvinist oratory, to the extent such reasoning is discernible it invalidates much more than sex-based strikes. After identifying unequal treatment (by separating individual exercises of peremptory challenge from the process as a whole), the Court applies the "heightened scrutiny" mode of equal-protection analysis used for sex-based discrimination, and concludes that the strikes fail heightened scrutiny because they do not substantially further an important government interest. The Court says that the only important government interest that could be served by peremptory strikes is "securing a fair and impartial jury." It refuses to accept respondent's argument that these strikes further that interest by eliminating a group (men) which may be partial to male defendants, because it will not accept any argument based on "'the very stereotype the law condemns.'" This analysis, entirely eliminating the only allowable argument, implies that sex-based strikes do not even rationally further a legitimate government interest, let alone pass heightened scrutiny. That places all peremptory strikes based on any group characteristic at risk, since they can all be denominated "stereotypes." Perhaps, however (though I do not see why it should be so), only the stereotyping of groups entitled to heightened or strict scrutiny constitutes "the very stereotype the law condemns"—so that other stereotyping (e.g., wide-eyed blondes and football players are dumb) remains OK. Or perhaps when the Court refers to "impermissible stereotypes," it means the adjective to be limiting rather than descriptive—so that we can expect to learn from the Court's peremptory/stereotyping jurisprudence in the future which stereotypes the Constitution frowns upon and which it does not. . . .

In order, it seems to me, not to eliminate any real denial of equal protection, but simply to pay conspicuous obeisance to the equality of the sexes, the Court imperils a practice that has been considered an essential part of fair jury trial since the dawn of the common law. The Constitution of the United States neither requires nor permits this vandalizing of our people's traditions.

For these reasons, I dissent.

INDEX OF CASES

Cases printed in boldface are excerpted on the page printed in boldface.